WEST INDIAN
TALES OF OLD

ADMIRAL JOHN BENBOW
From an engraving after the painting by Sir Godfrey Kneller

WEST INDIAN
TALES OF OLD

BY
Sir ALGERNON E. *Edward* ASPINALL

AUTHOR OF

"THE POCKET GUIDE TO THE WEST INDIES" AND "THE BRITISH
WEST INDIES: THEIR HISTORY, RESOURCES AND PROGRESS"

ILLUSTRATED

NEGRO UNIVERSITIES PRESS
NEW YORK

Originally Published in 1915
by Duckworth and Co.

Reprinted 1969 by
Negro Universities Press
A DIVISION OF GREENWOOD PUBLISHING CORP.
NEW YORK

Library of Congress Catalogue Card Number 69-18650

PREFACE

THE Caribbean Sea, which has been aptly described as the cockpit of the Empire, will shortly undergo a striking change. From being a mere cul-de-sac it will, now that the Panama Canal is completed, become one of the world's principal ocean highways and trade routes. One result of this will certainly be that an increasing number of visitors will patronise the British West Indian islands, and it occurred to me that it might be an opportune moment to re-tell, for their benefit, some of the tales connected with the West Indies, whose history is surrounded by a wealth of romance. Such is the origin of the present volume, in the compilation of which I have received much valuable assistance from Mr. N. Darnell Davis, C.M.G., the Hon. Arthur W. Holmes à Court, Mr. Cecil Headlam, Mr. Edgar Tripp, Mr. F. Sterns-Fadelle, Mr. Oscar Plummer, Mr. G. H. King, and other kind friends to whom I desire to express my indebtedness.

A. E. A.

CONTENTS

WEST INDIAN TALES OF OLD

CHAPTER I

BENBOW THE BRAVE

Come all you sailors bold
Lend an ear, lend an ear;
Come all you sailors bold lend an ear.
'Tis of our Admiral's fame,
Brave Benbow call'd by name;
How he fought on the main
You shall hear, you shall hear.

FROM AN OLD CHAUNTIE.

WHEN Admiral John Benbow was in Jamaica, Kingston, the present capital of the island, had only recently come into existence. Spanish Town—the old St. Iago de la Vega of the days of the first colonisers from Spain—was the chief town, and for many years Port Royal, formerly called Caguaya, at the extremity of the spit of sand which shelters what is now Kingston Harbour, had been the principal trade centre. Being conveniently situated it was much frequented by the members of that roving band of freebooters known as the buccaneers, who made it the storehouse and mart of their ill-gotten wealth, and the scene of the wildest excesses when they returned from their marauding expeditions.

But in 1692 a terrible calamity befell this proud

1

city. On June 7 in that year it was overwhelmed by
an earthquake, which threw down houses, churches and
nearly every building in the place. The event was
graphically described by the Rector, whose account of
it was published in a pamphlet, of which a copy is to
be seen in the British Museum. This worthy tells how
on the fateful day he had been at church reading
prayers as—he was careful to add—he did every day
"to keep up some show of religion among a most
ungodly and debauched people." After partaking of
a glass of wormwood wine—a beverage which still
forms the basis of that seductive Barbadian cock-
tail called " green bitters "—with the President of the
Council "as a whet before dinner " at a place frequented
by the merchants, he was sitting with him while he
smoked his pipe when the catastrophe occurred.

Though it is not altogether relevant to the story of
Benbow, what happened shall be described in the
Rector's own words. "I found the ground rolling and
moving under my feet," he states; "upon which I said
to him [the President] 'Lord, Sir, what is that?' He
replied, being a very grave man, 'It is an earthquake;
be not afraid, it will soon be over.' But it increased,
and we heard the church and tower fall, upon which
we ran to save ourselves; I quickly lost him and made
towards Morgan's fort, because being a wide, open
place, I thought to be there securest from the falling
houses; but as I made towards it, I saw the earth open
and swallow up a multitude of people, and the sea
mounting in upon them over the fortifications. I then
laid aside all thought of escaping, and resolved to make

2

toward my own lodging, and there to meet death in
as good posture as I could. From the place where I
was, I was forc'd to cross and run through two or three
very narrow streets, the houses and walls fell on each
side of me, some bricks came rowling over my shoes,
but none hurt me; when I came to my lodging I
found there all things in the same order I left them,
not a picture, of which there were several fair ones in
my chamber, being out of its place. I went to my
balcony to view the street in which our house stood, and
saw never a house down there, nor the ground so much
as cracked; the people seeing me there cry'd out
to me to come and pray with them; when I came
into the street every one laid hold on my cloaths and
embraced me, that with their fear and kindness I was
almost stifled; I persuaded them at least to kneel
down and make a large ring, which they did. I prayed
with them near an hour, when I was almost spent with
the heat of the sun, and the exercise; they then brought
me a chair, the earth working all the while with new
motions, and tremblings, like the rowlings of the sea;
insomuch that sometimes when I was at prayer I could
hardly keep myself upon my knees. By that time, I
had been half an hour longer with them in setting
before them their sins and heinous provocations and
in seriously exhorting them to repentance, there came
some merchants to me of the place, who desired me to
go aboard some ship in the harbour, and refresh myself,
telling me that they had gotten a boat to carry me off;
so coming to the sea, which had entirely swallowed up the
wharf with all those goodly brick houses upon it, most

of them as fine as those in Cheapside, and two intire
streets beyond that; I, upon the tops of some houses
which lay levelled with the surface of the water, got
first into a canoe, and then into a long boat, which put
me aboard a ship called the *Storm-Merchant*, where I
found the President safe, who was overjoyed to see
me; there I continued that night, but could not sleep
for the returns of the earthquake almost every hour,
which made all the guns in the ship to jarr and rattle.
The next day I went from ship to ship to visit those
that were bruised, and a dying, and to pray with them,
and likewise to do the last office at the sinking of several
corps that came floating from the point, which indeed
hath been my sorrowful employment ever since I came
aboard this ship with design to come for England, we
having nothing but shakings of the earth, and thunder
and lightening and foul weather ever since; and the
people being so desperately wicked it makes me afraid
to stay in the place; for that very day this terrible
earthquake was, as soon as night came on, a company
of lewd rogues whom they call privateers, fell to breaking open warehouses and houses deserted, to rob and
rifle their neighbours whilst the earth trembled under
them, and some of the houses fell on them in the act:
And those audacious whores that remain still upon the
place are as impudent and drunken as ever. I have
been twice on shoar to pray with the bruised and
dying people, and to christen children, where I met
too many drunk and swearing; I did not spare them,
nor the magistrates neither, who have suffered wickedness to grow to so great a height; I have I bless God

4

to the best of my skill and power discharged my duty
in this place, which you will hear from most persons
that come from hence ; I have preached so seasonably
to them, and so plain in the last sermon I preached to
them in the church : I set before them what would be
the issue of their impenitence, and wickedness, that
they have since confessed that it was more like a
prophesie than a sermon ; I had, I confess, an impulse
on me to do it : And many times I have preached in
this pulpit, things that I never premeditated at home,
and could not methought do otherwise. The day when
all this befel us was very clear, afforded not the suspicion
of the least evil ; but in the space of three minutes,
about half an hour after eleven in the morning,
Port Royal, the fairest town of all the English
plantations, the best emporium and mart of this part
of the world, exceeding in its riches, plentiful of all
good things, was shaken and shattered to pieces, and
sunk into, and covered for the greatest part, by the sea
and will in a short time be wholly eaten up by it ; for
few of those houses that yet stand are left whole, and
every day we hear them fall, and the sea daily
encroaches upon it ; we guess, that by the falling of
the houses and the opening of the earth and the
inundation of the waters, there are lost fifteen hundred
persons and many of good note."

In a later letter the Rector tells how " whole streets
were swallowed up by the opening earth, and the
houses and inhabitants went down together, some
of them were driven up again by the sea, which arose
in those breaches and wonderfully escaped ; some were

swallowed up to the neck, and then the earth shut upon them, and squeezed them to death; and in that manner several are left buried with their heads above ground, only some heads the dogs have eaten, others are covered with dust and earth by the people which yet remain in the place to avoid the stench."

To what extent the Rector's account is a true portrayal of the catastrophe must remain a matter of conjecture; but it is worthy of note that the inscription on the tomb of one Lewis Galdy, at Green Bay, across Kingston Harbour, records how that individual "was swallowed up by the earthquake, and by the providence of God was, by another shock, thrown into the sea, and miraculously saved by swimming until a boat took him up," and how "he lived many years after in great reputation, beloved by all who knew him, and much lamented at his death."

That Port Royal never recovered from the effects of the earthquake of 1692 is not to be wondered at. The greater part of the town was swallowed up, and, unlike Lewis Galdy, it has never since been disgorged. A buoy, inscribed "Church Buoy," floats over the spot where it is believed the old church stood, and some people declare that on a calm day the ruins of the edifice can be seen below the pellucid waters of the harbour. The dockyard is now practically deserted, and beyond the officers' quarters, with their trim lawn at each corner of which is a gaudily painted figure-head of one of our old wooden walls, and the historic and exceedingly picturesque Fort Charles where Nelson commanded in 1779, the town has few attractions.

BENBOW THE BRAVE

Within a very short time after the destruction of Port Royal, the Council decided to build a new town on what they then believed would be a safer site, and instructions were issued for a survey to be made of two hundred acres of land in the parish of St. Andrew's on the northernmost shore of the magnificent sheet of water enclosed by the spit of land already referred to, which is called the Palisadoes. A few days later they ordered that £1000 should be paid to the owner, who was William Beeston, Lieutenant Governor of Jamaica from 1693 to 1700, and Governor from that year until 1702.

For several years Kingston was little more than a collection of temporary huts which sheltered the comparatively few survivors from Port Royal. Sir Hans Sloane, the distinguished naturalist and founder of the British Museum, who went to Jamaica in 1687, in the suite of Christopher Monck, second Duke of Albemarle, the autocratic Governor of the island for a brief year, quotes a letter dated July 3rd, 1693, in which reference is made to the new town, from which it would appear that it was an extremely unhealthy spot. "Others," the letter runs, "went to the place called Kingston (or by others Killcown) where from the first clearing of the ground, and from bad accommodations, then hutts built with boughs, and not sufficient to keep out rain, which in great and an unusual manner followed the earthquake, lying wet, and wanting medicines, and all conveniences, etc., they died miserably in heaps. Indeed there was a general sickness (supposed to proceed from the hurtful vapours belch'd from the many openings of the Earth) all over the island so general that few

7

escaped being sick; and 'tis thought it swept away in all parts of the island 3000 souls; the greatest part from Kingston only, yet an unhealthy place."

Little attempt seems to have been made to lay out the town on any organised plan until the year 1695, when the assistance of Colonel Christian Lilly, the famous military engineer, was invoked. Colonel Lilly first went out to the West Indies in 1692—the year of the Port Royal earthquake—with a train of brass ordnance and mortars. He took part in Sir F. Wheeler's expedition to Barbados, Martinique, the Leeward Islands, New England and Newfoundland in command of an artillery train and after seeing active service in San Domingo he was stationed in Jamaica in 1695. The Council were fortunate in being able to avail themselves of the services of so eminent an engineer.

Under Lilly's guidance the mean huts of Kingston soon gave way to more substantial structures, and the town was rapidly constructed on the present rectangular plan, with the parish church, or, at any rate, a space for the church, in the centre. When the church was actually completed, is not known; but it is certain that it must have been standing in Benbow's time, for the earliest tomb bears the date 1699, while some of the Communion plate is dated 1701.

By an irony of fate Kingston, which owed its existence to an earthquake, was, as all the world knows, to a great extent destroyed by a similar visitation, which was accompanied by a devastating fire, in 1907.

That appalling disaster is of such comparatively recent occurrence that it will suffice to remind the reader

KINGSTON PARISH CHURCH IN 1844
From an old engraving

THE PARISH CHURCH AT KINGSTON JAMAICA

how, on a brilliantly fine day in January, when the
tourist season was at its height, the town was full
of visitors and sightseers. A conference of delegates
gathered from every part of the West Indies, and
augmented by an influential party of guests from
England, brought out by that generous shipowner, the
late Sir Alfred Jones, was sitting in the old Mico
College buildings, in Hanover Street, when Kingston was
shaken to its foundations by an earthquake. When
the clouds of dust had cleared away, it was found that
a raging fire was completing the work of destruction.

On this occasion no suggestion was made of altering
the site of the city, and the work of rebuilding Kingston
has since proceeded apace. It is indeed already possible
to appreciate what a handsome capital Jamaica will have
when the work is completed, as it will be in a few years'
time. The streets are wide, and far cleaner than of old,
while gardens already green with turf and bright with
flowering trees and palms delight the eye and refresh the
senses.

The old wooden and brick buildings have been replaced
by structures of reinforced concrete, and it is a revelation
to visitors to find what picturesque houses can be constructed from such common-place materials. Some of
the new buildings have domes and others flat roofs,
which give the city quite an Oriental appearance, and it
is very generally conceded that architecturally, as well
as from an hygienic point of view, the new Kingston is
an infinitely more attractive city than its somewhat
ramshackle predecessor.

Like nearly every other building in the city which

was not actually destroyed, the old Parish Church suffered severely from the earthquake. It was indeed so badly damaged that it had practically to be reconstructed. The picturesque old tower which used to stand at the west end was no longer safe and had to be demolished, and an extension of the nave now covers its site. Apart, however, from this alteration the church has been restored on its original lines, the only modifications introduced being those rendered necessary through the substitution of reinforced concrete for bricks and mortar and the desirability of protecting the building from the effects of any future seismic disturbance.

It is a matter for regret that the handsome Baldacchino which graced the chancel from the beginning of the nineteenth century has been sacrificed to modern " taste," and still more it is to be deplored that many of the mural tablets and tombstones should have been irretrievably ruined. The most treasured of all of the latter has, however, fortunately escaped almost unblemished.

This is a simple slab of bluish grey slate within the chancel rails. Every English visitor should gaze upon it with reverence, for it is the tombstone of the redoubtable John Benbow. It bears the following inscription :

> HERE LYETH INTERRED THE
> BODY OF JOHN BENBOW
> ESQ. ADMIRAL OF THE WHITE
> A TRUE PATTERN OF ENGLISH

BENBOW THE BRAVE

Courage who Lost his life
In Defence of his Queene
& Country November Y^e 4th
1702 In the 52^d year of
his Age by A wound In his Legg
Receiued In an Engagement
with Monsr Du Casse Being
much lamented.

According to some authorities, Benbow, who was
born in 1653, was the son of a tanner of Shrewsbury;
others, however, declare that his father was a butcher,
and that it was from the parental shop that he ran
away to sea. His uncle was Captain John Benbow
who, after serving with the Parliamentary forces,
espoused the Royalist cause on the death of the King,
and being captured at the battle of Worcester, was
tried by court-martial and shot.

Young Benbow's early years were passed partly in
the navy, which he joined in 1678, and partly in the
merchant service. In the latter his career was most
adventurous, and the story is told how, on one
occasion, when he was owner of a vessel employed in
the Levant trade, he rounded up some Moorish pirates
to the number of thirteen and cut off their heads.
These he then salted and took to the astonished magistrates at Cadiz, from whom he demanded and was
successful in obtaining a reward.

After the revolution Benbow re-entered the navy,
and he had already occupied the positions of master-
attendant at Chatham Dockyard and at Deptford,

11

master-of-the-fleet at Beachy Head, Barfleur and the
Hague and commandant of a flotilla of bomb-vessels
against the French when in 1697-8 he was appointed
commander-in-chief of the King's ships in the West
Indies, with instructions to suppress piracy in the
Caribbean Sea.

Reaching Barbados in February 1698–9, and finding
all quiet there, he at once proceeded to Cartagena on
the Spanish Main. By threats of a blockade, he
persuaded the governor of that city to release two
English vessels, which he was detaining with the object
of using them for the purpose of an expedition against
the Scotch colony at Darien—a colony founded by a
company which had been granted extensive powers by
an Act of the Scottish Parliament in 1695 and proved
eventually a dismal failure.

Benbow then went after the pirates, whom he
hunted from pillar to post, spreading consternation
in their ranks. Some took refuge under the Danish flag
at St. Thomas, while others left West Indian waters
altogether, only to return when he sailed again for
England in 1700.

On his arrival in the Channel, Benbow was now
given the command in the Downs, and after holding
that appointment for a while, and serving as Vice-
Admiral of the Blue, under Sir George Rooke, who
afterwards achieved fame by capturing Gibraltar for
Queen Anne, he was once again destined to visit the
West Indies.

War with France was imminent, and there was need
of an able commander in the Caribbean. The choice

12

ADMIRAL BENBOW'S TOMB
In the Parish Church, Kingston, Jamaica

fell on Benbow; but King William III thinking it ungenerous to send him back so soon to such an unfavourable station, first offered the appointment to other admirals of distinction who, however, preferred the dress and pleasures of London to risking their lives in a tropical climate, and consequently declined. Thereupon the King is alleged to have said : " Well then, I find we must spare our *beaux* and send our honest Benbow."

Benbow accordingly hoisted his flag on board the *Breda*, a vessel of 70 guns, and sailed from Spithead for the West Indies at the end of August 1701, being escorted as far as the Scillies by Sir George Rooke, and then for some days' sail to westward of the Azores by Sir John Munden's squadron.

He arrived at Barbados on November 3, and finding the Leeward Islands in a good state of defence he proceeded immediately to Jamaica and dropped anchor off Port Royal on December 5.

Towards the end of January 1702 Benbow heard, from the captains of some vessels which had been sent out as a reinforcement, of the arrival at Martinique of a French force of superior strength to his own, under the command of M. Château Renaud, whose object was believed to be an attack on Barbados and the Leeward Islands. In March the further news reached him that a Spanish squadron under the Marquis de Coetlogon had succeeded in effecting a juncture with the French, that the combined fleet had put to sea and that Monsieur Du Casse, the new French Governor of Léogane in Hispaniola, was momentarily expected to arrive from Europe " to

13

settle the Assiento," or contract for the supply of negro slaves for the plantations and mines, "and destroy the trade of the English and Dutch on that coast."

In July the tidings reached Barbados that war with France had been declared, and Benbow at once decided to act on the offensive. For a while he cruised off the coast of Hispaniola where he met with a few small successes. Then he heard that a French squadron of four sail of the line of 60 to 70 guns apiece, one large frigate and several smaller vessels under the command of Monsieur Du Casse was escorting the Governor—the Duke of Albuquerque—to Mexico. On receiving this intelligence he immediately started off in the *Breda* to intercept them with a squadron consisting of the *Defiance*, Captain Richard Kirkby; the *Windsor*, Captain John Constable; the *Greenwich*, Captain John Wade; the *Ruby*, Captain George Walton; the *Pendennis*, Captain Thomas Hudson; and the *Falmouth*, Captain Thomas Vincent.

The two squadrons came within sight of one another on August 19 at a distance of about twelve miles from Santa Marta on the Spanish Main, now a busy port o Colombia, from which millions of bananas are shipped to Europe every year. Benbow at once made the signal for battle; but the French held on their course, and only one or two broadsides were exchanged. At nightfall Du Casse made off, closely pursued by the *Breda* and *Ruby*, while the remaining English vessels held aloof. The admiral sent to Kirkby and ordered him to make more sail and get abreast of the enemy's van; but he declined to do so, and after firing a few broadsides

14

luffed up out of the line and out of gun-shot. On the three following days the pursuit was maintained by the *Breda* and the *Ruby*, the only other vessel which joined in the chase being the *Falmouth*. On August 21 the French, seeing the English vessels isolated, shortened sail and showed fight. A sharp engagement followed, during which the *Defiance* came up without, however, firing a single shot. Two days later Benbow engaged the entire French squadron single-handed, and succeeded in recapturing the *Anne*, a British galley which had been taken by the French, and sent her with the *Ruby*, which was disabled, to Jamaica.

On August 24, at 2 A.M. the *Breda* came within hail of the sternmost French ship, and at once opened fire. Supported now by the *Falmouth* Benbow delivered a broadside which was responded to with vigour, and three times on that memorable day did the valiant Admiral board the French flagship before his leg was shattered to pieces by a chain-shot. This occurred at 3 AM., and Benbow was carried below; but he refused to remain there, and insisted upon being taken to the quarter-deck whence he continued to direct operations. "The admiral, not at all discouraged," wrote Lieut.-Governor Beckford to the Earl of Nottingham, "order'd his cradle upon the quarter-deck, and gave the signall for his Fleet to fall into a line of battle, and fall upon the enemy."

"I am sorry, sir," said Fogg, his captain, "to see you in this state."

"I am sorry too," replied Benbow, "but I would rather have lost both legs than have seen this disgrace

15

brought on the British flag." To quote Governor Beckford again : " Never was poor gent certainly so disserted by a parcell of . . . unworthy I think of being ever trusted again with a further command."

The French flagship was now in a pitiable condition. Her mainmast was shot to pieces, her fore-top-sail yard was shot away, her mizzen-mast had gone by the board, her rigging was reduced to a mass of tangled cordage, and her sides pierced through and through by the shot.

Victory must have been Benbow's but for the poltroonery of the captains, who still resolutely declined to engage. Kirkby seeing the ship disabled bore down on her with the other vessels ; but, thinking better of it, he sailed away again, and the other dastardly captains followed his example.

Throughout the action the *Breda* only had the support of the *Falmouth*, the other vessels remaining well out of range of the enemy's guns. The French taking advantage of Benbow's isolation succeeded in recapturing a prize which they had lost earlier in the fight and sailed off with her. The *Breda's* rigging was by now so shattered that it was not until two o'clock in the afternoon that sufficient repairs had been carried out to put her in a position to start in pursuit of the enemy. Fogg, the captain of the *Breda*, was then sent to order his cowardly colleagues to keep the line of battle, and to behave like Englishmen and to join in the pursuit ; whereupon Kirkby to Benbow's chagrin came aboard the flagship, and without so much as asking after the admiral's health, earnestly begged that the pursuit might be abandoned.

BENBOW THE BRAVE

The other captains were summoned and Benbow, " who then lay in a cradle on the orelope deck," did his utmost to prevail upon them to withdraw their opposition to his plans. He pointed out that their masts and yards were in good condition, that few men save in his own ship the *Breda* had been killed, and that the opportunity for vanquishing the enemy was a fair one. Nothing, however, would persuade the captains to change their determination to support Kirkby in the contemptible attitude which he had adopted. Benbow was, therefore, at last reluctantly compelled to give way, and returned crestfallen to Jamaica.

Kirkby, who was undoubtedly the ringleader in this despicable affair, was next in seniority to Benbow, and it may be that his actions were prompted by jealousy. He had not a good name in the navy. Before he was gazetted to the *Defiance* he had been captain of the *Southampton*, a vessel in which the discipline was decidedly lax. Floggings were of constant occurrence, and Kirkby's methods of endeavouring to restore order were very drastic. One seaman was sentenced to be " towed ashore," in consequence of his " scandalous actions to the great corruption of good manners "; another was punished by being tied up by his right arm and left leg for several hours. On returning from the West Indies in 1689, Kirkby himself was tried on a charge of embezzling, plunder, cruelty and oppression, but was acquitted.

Benbow was heart-broken at victory having been

17

snatched from him. In a letter to his wife he wrote that the loss of his leg did not trouble him half so much as the villainous treachery of some of the captains, which hindered him from totally destroying the French squadron,*. and it is said that he received from Du Casse a letter couched in the following terms:

" SIR,

" I had little hopes on Monday last but to have supped in your cabin; it pleased God to order it otherwise. I am thankful for it. As for those cowardly captains who deserted you, hang them up, for by God they deserve it !

" Yours,

" DU CASSE."

The authenticity of this letter is more than doubtful; but it is reasonable to suppose that the trenchant comments attributed to Du Casse accurately expressed the feelings which must have been in the breast of the French commander. The French squadron after its fortunate and quite unlooked for escape, made the best of its way back to Cartagena. After refitting there it returned to Europe, barely eluding on the voyage the attentions of Vice-Admiral Graydon, who pursued it and engaged the sternmost ship.

Upon arriving at Port Royal, Benbow at once ordered Admiral Whetstone, who had joined him in the station, to hold a court-martial for the trial ot

* " A Chronological History of West Indies," by Captain Thomas Southey, R.N.

captains for cowardice, breach of orders and neglect of duty. This Whetstone was a son of John Whetstone, master of William Penn's flagship the *Swiftsure* during the expedition of 1655, which resulted in the capture of Jamaica.

The court - martial was accordingly opened on board *H.M.S. Breda* off Port Royal, on October 8. It lasted for four days. The charges against Captain Kirkby of the *Defiance* were proved on the oaths of the admiral, ten commissioned officers, and eleven warrant and inferior officers. In the evidence it was shown that during the six days' engagement he not only failed to encourage his men to fight, but showed an exceedingly bad example, "dodging behind the mizen-mast, and falling down on deck at the noise of a shot." Moreover, it was stated that he amended the master of the ship's journal of the transactions of the fight to suit his own ends. When asked why he did not fire at the enemy's stern-most ship he repeatedly replied that it was because they did not fire at him, " for that they had a respect for him." He wrote a long letter to the Secretary of the Admiralty alleging that Benbow's injudicious and ignorant conduct was the real cause of defeat, and that the court-martial was ordered by the admiral to divert attention from his own faults ; but in spite of this he was sentenced to be shot.

Captain Constable of the *Windsor* was exonerated from the charge of cowardice on the evidence of his own officers and men. He called several witnesses to prove that he remained on the quarter-deck through-out the engagement and encouraged his men to fight and "sometimes gave them drams of rum," but he was found guilty of breach of orders and neglect of duty and was sentenced to be cashiered and to be imprisoned during her Majesty's pleasure. The charges against Wade of the *Greenwich*, who was the next captain to be tried, were proved on the evidence of sixteen commissioned and warrant officers of his own ship and by several others, who deposed that during the six days' engagement he never kept the line of battle but fired his shot uselessly and was "in drink" when he signed the paper. He was sentenced to share the same fate as Kirkby.

Captain Vincent of the *Falmouth* and Captain Fogg of the flagship were then put on their trial for signing the document with Kirkby and the other officers against engaging the French when there was "so fine an opportunity and probability of success." They pleaded in justification of their action that they feared that if they did not sign the captains might on some future occasion desert entirely and leave the *Breda* and the *Falmouth* a prey to the French. This defence was so far accepted that upon the evidence given by Benbow, who was himself present in court, and others of their great courage and gallant behaviour in the battle, the court only ordered that they should be suspended during her Majesty's pleasure.

Captain Hudson of the *Pendennis* was spared the ignominy of being tried by court-martial, as he died before his trial and so escaped the punishment which he so richly deserved.

Kirkby and Wade were sent back to England in the *Bristol* in charge of Captain Edward Acton, and were executed on board that vessel in Plymouth Sound on April 10, 1703, without being permitted even to set foot on English soil again.

Benbow did not survive to learn that effect had been given to the judgment of the court. Shattered in health through the loss of his leg he succumbed to an attack of fever on November 4, 1702. So passed away a valiant and able commander.

There is a tradition, the origin of which cannot be traced, that Benbow's body was brought home to England, and that it was laid to rest in the churchyard of St. Nicholas, Deptford "at the north-west angle formed by the projection of the steeple beyond the body of the church." It is difficult to understand how this belief can have arisen, for there is certainly no evidence existing on which it could have been based. Another tradition makes Greenwich, then a naval station in the harbour to the west of Kingston, Benbow's place of interment, and in support of it is the fact that under date November 5, 1702, the burial of " Admiral John Bembo" is recorded in the register of Halfway Tree Church, St. Andrews—the same parish as that in which Greenwich was and is situated. On the other hand, the tombstone in the parish church of Kingston makes it clear that it was there that the brave admiral was buried. Those who doubt this might, however, point out that the inscription on the slate slab is in several respects inaccurate. When he died he was not 51, as stated on the tombstone, but 49 years old. Again, he was Admiral of the Blue and not of the White. It is also claimed that the coat-of-arms on the tombstone which

21

is heraldically described : " Palewise between two sheaves of arrows two bent bows. Crest on an esquire's helmet a harpy," is not that of Benbow. But even nowadays mistakes in monumental inscriptions are not infrequently perpetrated, and it is possible that the inaccuracies on Benbow's tomb had their origin in a mason's yard in England, and that, when the discrepancy was discovered, it was not considered desirable for the stone to be sent across the sea again for a correction to be made.

The writer at any rate is satisfied that the pilgrim desirous of visiting the heroic Benbow's tomb, will find it in that simple slab in the old Parish Church of Kingston.

CHAPTER II

THE FATE OF GOVERNOR PARKE

WEST Indians have not infrequently been afflicted by having governors set over them who have been altogether unsuited to control the destinies of a tropical country, and who, by lack of tact and by their overbearing manner, have rendered themselves thoroughly disliked by all classes of the communities.

Numerous instances could, indeed, be cited of West Indian governors, in the past, whose unpopularity has been such that their recall has been imperative in the interest of order and of public safety. Fortunately, however, the people in the West Indies when anxious to rid themselves of a tyrannous governor, have rarely been compelled to take the law into their own hands, so extreme a step being generally obviated by the peculiar custom which used to prevail of promoting unsuccessful officials to other colonies.

It was quite otherwise, however, with Daniel Parke, the Governor in Chief and Captain General of the Leeward Islands in the days of Queen Anne, as the following pages will show.

As an official Governor Parke was a hopeless failure.

As a private individual he had a character which did not bear investigation. Born in Virginia of obscure parents in 1669, Parke first came into prominence by marrying a wealthy lady, of respectable family, whom he is said to have treated disgracefully. After robbing her of her fortune he deserted her, and we next hear of him committing a crime at the gaming tables in one of the northern states and fleeing to England to escape punishment. Here he purchased an estate at Whitchurch, in Hampshire, and was returned to Parliament as a member for the borough. It was not long, however, before he was expelled from the House of Commons for bribery, and instructions were issued for his prosecution, but, through the intervention of the Earl of Pembroke, he managed to elude trial.

His next action was to form a *liaison* with the wife of a captain in the Guards. To escape the vengeance of the enraged husband, he left England and fled to Holland, where he entered the English army, under John Churchill, the illustrious Duke of Marlborough Becoming the Duke's aide-de-camp, it was soon afterwards his good fortune to be entrusted with the duty of conveying to Queen Anne and to the Duchess the news of the victory of Blenheim, on August 2, 1704.

This stroke of luck proved to be the turning point in Parke's career, for his handsome appearance and soldierly bearing commended themselves to the Queen, who undertook to reward him for his services. If we are to believe Parke's despatches he was indeed promised the government of Virginia. "The Duke," he wrote, in one of his letters to the Lords Commissioners for Trade

H: Excelleney Daniel Parke Esq.ʳ Cap.ᵗ Gen.
Chiefe Governour of the Leward Island.
Ætat Suæ 41. Ob. 7 Decemb.ʳ 1710.

DANIEL PARKE

Governor-in-Chief and Captain-General of the Leeward
Islands 1706–1710

—the predecessors of the Secretary of State for the Colonies—" promised me the government of Virginia at the battle of Blenheim, but, for some reasons of State, that was given to my Lord Orkney." No doubt these " reasons" were that General Lord George Hamilton, the first Earl of Orkney, had achieved distinction in the battle, commanding a brigade of infantry, and taking no fewer than thirteen hundred officers and twelve thousand men prisoners in the village of Blenheim, a feat the like of which Parke certainly never performed. It was not until early in 1706 that Queen Anne took the opportunity of rewarding the messenger, who had brought her such good tidings, with a government; though she had already, it is said, presented him with her portrait richly set with diamonds and a purse of one thousand guineas. In that year the governorship of the Leeward Caribbee Islands fell vacant through the death of Sir William Matthew (a native of St. Kitts, who had distinguished himself at the siege of Namur), and Parke, tired of waiting for preferment, applied for the post.

Colonel Christopher Codrington—the founder of that picturesque college in Barbados which bears his name, and the benefactor of All Souls, Oxford—who had been Governor in succession to his father from 1700 to 1704 when he was recalled, also sought the position, and his application was warmly supported by the Lords Commissioners of Trade, but Parke, who now enjoyed the Queen's favour, proved a stronger candidate and received the appointment.

Parke was anxious to reach Antigua, which was then,

as now, the seat of government of the Leeward Islands, without delay ; but for months no ship was available, a circumstance which irritated him considerably, and it was not until July 14, 1706, that he arrived at St. John's, the capital of the island, where he was received with due ceremony and every sign of popular approval.

From the outset he seems to have taken a cordial dislike to the place and its inhabitants and we find him in his despatches giving vent to his feelings in no uncertain manner. To begin with, he complained that the troops at his disposal, which consisted of 928 men of the Queen's regiment, were quite insufficient to defend the island ; and when it became necessary for him to visit Nevis, which had just been ravaged by the French, he wrote : "I will take all the soldiers and be with them myself. I will run the same fate with them if I have my brains knock't out, the Queen must send some other unfortunate devil here to be roasted in the sun."

Again, he averred that the "islands are too small, they will not maintain inhabitants enough to defend them," and he suggested that the only way to relieve the situation would be by destroying Martinique or taking "Porto Rico (it is a large healthy island) with a view to the inhabitants being removed to it and settling there." What, one wonders, would the good people of the Leeward Islands, who so dearly love their home, say, at the present day, if they were told that they would have to remove bag and baggage to a neighbouring island ?

Not a packet reached England from Antigua without a despatch from Parke making some complaint, whether it was regarding his very inadequate salary, the people

of the island, or the climate. " I have," he wrote, " the
least salary of the Queen's Governors, except Bermudas
. . . and . . . have four times the trouble, having four
Governments, each Island being a separate Government.
I receive but eleaven hundred pounds in mony from the
Treasury, and that not paid as my Agent informs me,
all my perquisites I lett at sixty pounds sterling pr
annum and he that rents it will not give it another year,
this with what the Islands allowes me for my house is
what I have comeing in all manner of wages, I am
forced to keep two houses, one at Antigua and another
at St. Christophers; everything is so very dear. I can
hardly live uppon my income ; and yet I never lived
worse in all my life ; I came over twenty six in family,
there is now but four left, five indeed are gone for
England, the rest are dead; I myself have had the
plague, the pestilence and bloody flux, and have been
out of my bed but four days of a malignant feavour ; I
am so weak I can hardly write to your Lordships ; could
I have foreseen what I was to suffer, and how little 'twas
possible for me to gett ; I would never have come over ;
I should not think your Lordships sallery to much were
it three times as much as 'tis, but can't but think myself
very unhappy that your Lordships should think mine
too great, considering I have no more than my predecessor and much less than I was promised when I had the
Commission given me ; the Duke promised me the
Government of Virginia at the Battle of Blenheim, but
for some reasons of State that was given to my Lord
Orkney and this given to me with a promise the sallery
should be the same which is two thousand pounds

sterling the year, I find myself mistaken and at this distance forgot. All my predecessors have had complaints against them from some Island or other in less than six months after their arrivall, Collonel Codrington had severall in less than three : Sir William Matthew would have had one in less than three had he lived, for they were preparing one before he fell sick. I have been here above a year and I believe you will not be troubled with any publick complaint, except the people of Nevis complain that I took from them some gunns and armes they did not want, and carryed them to St. Johns where they were wanted I think 'tis my duty not to suffer the Queens stores to ly useless in one Island when they are very much wanted in another."

Of the inhabitants he said, "The people of Nevis expect the Queen should do everything for them, though they do not endeavour to help themselves," a failing which, it must be admitted, is even now characteristic of some residents in the West Indies.

Within a few months of assuming the reins of Government, Parke wrote to the Lords Commissioners : "When I brought the news, the Queen promised to provide for me; I had this post given me, 'twas a year before I could get transportation ; I was carryed to Barbados where I fell sick, I found my Government plundered ; I have had the plague, have four distinct governments, I must be a continual vagabond going from one to the other, Nevis being 18 leagues from Antegoa ; 1200L the year in a dear country ; I hope your Lordships will not envy, Your Lordships' obedient Humble Servant, Daniel Parke."

THE FATE OF GOVERNOR PARKE

"I would have allowed your Lordships more paper if I had had it. I had much ado to gett this, being found by the packet in a poor plundered Island; had the paper held out; to the rest of my afflictions, I would have added Colonel Codrington. I hope I shall do my duty and please the people till the Queen will provide for me better; I hope your Lordships will excuse what's amiss, for I am almost crased with the fateague, the hott weather, and my feaver, which I have been quitt of but three days. I compair my post to that of a serjeant with twelve men upon an advanc'd post; allways allarmed; We are so frighted, every two or three sloops, we believe is another French fleet, and I must mount tho' at midnight. I am deservedly punished for desiring to be a Governor."

Parke professed to believe, however, that he was quite popular and that he enjoyed the full confidence of the inhabitants of the islands with the exception of Christopher Codrington, who appears from the outset to have been his "hated rival" and a thorn in his side. "I think I have the good fortune to please the people," he modestly wrote, "except Colonel Codrington. He has opposed everything and is just as much troublesome as I told you he would be."

At first, no doubt, the glamour surrounding Parke's appointment—and it was known that he was a favourite of the Queen—led to the new Governor enjoying a certain degree of popularity; but this soon evaporated, and it was not long before the first rupture between him and the Legislature arose, the cause of it being the most flagrant abuse of his prerogative of patronage.

" Being a vulgar man," writes Mrs. Llanigan in "Antigua
and the Antiguans," "he delighted in vulgar associates."
One of these " vulgar associates " he appointed a member of the House of Assembly, and another, a private
soldier named Michael Ayon, he made Provost Marshal.
" Another crime of huge magnitude was the seduction
of Mrs. Chester, the wife of Edward Chester, Esq., one
of the most opulent of the Antiguan merchants and a
member of the House of Assembly." To add insult to
injury he then threw the injured husband into prison,
accusing him of the murder of a man who had been
accidentally killed. To quote Bryan Edwards, the West
Indian historian, " He feared neither God nor man;
and it was soon observed of him, as it had been of
another detestable tyrant, that he spared no man in his
anger nor woman in his lust."

Meanwhile the Legislature, impressed by Parke's
professed influence at Court, did what had never been
done before, and passed an Act " for raising the
quantity of one hundred thousand pounds of good
muscavado sugar per annm. for discharging the rent
of a house for the accommodation of His Excellency ";
but this did not satisfy the exacting Governor, and he
continued to complain bitterly of his inadequate salary
to the Lords Commissioners, whom he freely charged
with indifference to the welfare of the colonies.

On September 22nd he wrote : " I believe the
Ministry forgetts this part of the Queen's Dominions ;
or they would not suffer us to be thus insulted by the
Queen's enemy's; the French have five men of warr
(two of them of sixty odd gunns) at Martinique. The

swan is all we have and she (tho' there is a very good man in her) is so chill a sayler and of so small force that I am afraid she will be taken every time she goes out."

A drought which occurred soon after his arrival was another subject of complaint. During it "Water was sold as dear as good beer in London; everything else is four times as dear as 'tis in England."

Against the indifferent attitude of the people towards the then all-important matter of defence, he protested: "Whilst the fright lasted [when an invasion was expected] the people sent me negroes to fortifie Monks' Hill, but being over I can't gett a negroe to finish what I had begun, but they promise to do it when the crop is over."

To add to his discomfort, and to the difficulties of the situation with which he was endeavouring to cope, the islands under his care had the misfortune to be visited by a violent hurricane. The following is a description of that occurrence in Governor Parke's own words: "The people having made good cropps began to be in good humour and they had allmost forgot their losses by the French (which hap'ned to them just before I arrived) but to our great misfortune on the 29th of August last in the night we had a terrible storm which is called here a hurricane, Antigua has the least damage, yet they have suffered very much; but in St. Kitts, Nevis and Montserrat most of the houses are blown down, and those that stand are miserably shattered, for my own part I have lost allmost all I have ever since I came. I have been

31

building a house at St. Kitts which is now blown down and the floods have carryed away all the timber into the sea, I had hyred a plantation there, and am obliged to leave it in repaire which will cost me as much as one whole year's salary and perquisites comes to, all my furniture in my house in Antegoa is spoyld ; I do assure your Lordships I am now much a poorer man than when I came, which is very hard after having endured so much sickness and fateague.

" All the vessells in the harbour were drove ashore and one *Bristol* ship overset and lost ; the *Childs Play* Man of War drove on shore at St. Kitts and is lost, but the men all saved ; The *Winchelsea* was sent to convoy some vessells, she was seen that evening off St. Kitts, but has not been heard of since ; I am afraid she and all her men are lost; for there is come on shore at St. Bartholomews some part of the wrack of a great ship and one man drown'd which by description was the Captains Taylor. I have been ever since a prisoner in this Island for want of a vessell, but I have persuaded the inhabitants to fit out a sloope which I hope will be ready to sayle next week : as soon as she is ready I will visit the other Islands. This Island is at a very great expence in quartering of the soldiers, and since this misfortune the people begin to grumble very much, especially since there is no care taken as we hear of for the paying the soldiers, who have not received one farthing pay since they came. Everything is very dear, and if your Lordships does not procure us some nimble frigots to protect us from the privateers we shall all starve, for they are so numerous they will take all vessells bound to these Islands. We have expected the London fleet since July last, God send them safe to us, otherwise we shall be in a very miserable condition; if Her Majesty had any money to spare it would be very great charity in her to send us some provision and nayles, for to rebuild our houses."

It will be gathered that soon after his arrival in the colony Parke had his work cut out for him in repelling the French, who had been plundering St. Kitts and Nevis. He then set about endeavouring to effect much needed internal reforms, a policy which did not at all commend itself to the inhabitants. Ignoring their protests, Parke marshalled the small body of local troops at his disposal and attempted to awe the people by a show of force, but in this he was certainly not successful.

The grounds for complaint against the Governor, if not in every instance weighty, were numerous. To begin with it was claimed that, with the object of awing the people and reducing them to submission and servility, he had openly boasted that the Lord High Treasurer and the Duchess of Marlborough had promised their support and protection in whatever he did. Then he was charged with perverting the witnesses in a case in which Edward Chester, the man whom he had already wronged, was prosecuted for the murder of one Thomas Sawyer; and further, with inducing the coroner's inquest by threats to find that the murdered man was killed by a blow on the head with a tankard, though he really, as they were well aware, died a natural death.

What probably made the planters most angry was his challenging the titles by which they held their estates; and commanding "Col. Christopher Codrington, by a precept sign'd by the said Col. Parke, immediately upon sight . . . to give him the said General an account how, and by what authority, he the said Codrington did hold the island of Barbuda." Inasmuch as Codrington's father and uncle had been in the undisturbed possession of the island for upwards of twenty-five years, and held it by several patents, those planters less secure in the ownership of their estates naturally felt alarmed at the prospect which Governor Parke's action opened up.

Then Parke was accused of neglecting the defences of the island. It appears that when the French fleet was in the neighbourhood he withdrew the troops, ammunition and provisions from the fort at Monk's Hill, which had only recently been built at immense cost for the protection of women and children and valuable property in the event of invasion, and entrenched and fortified the town of St. John's instead, an arrangement which did not at all suit the residents.

In defence of his conduct in this respect, Parke referred to a report made by Colonel Christian Lilly on March 24, 1707, in which that expert declared that "there is no such thing in the whole country as deserves the name of a fort; for that which is built upon *Monk's Hill* is not so, since an enemy upon his first landing, without having occasion to bring any cannon against it, may easily make himself master of it with sword in hand: nor can this place in my opinion be

34

well fortify'd without a very great deal of unnecessary expence." This eminent engineer further asserted that it had been "contriv'd and delineated contrary to one of the most fundamental rules and maxims in the art of fortification; which requires that all the ports of a fort should mutually flank and defend one another." "Upon all which considerations," he concluded, "I do hereby utterly condemn Monk's Hill as unfit to be further proceeded upon."

Parke was further charged with using his position as Chancellor to flout the laws of the island, and of having committed various offences against the Customs regulations. His appointments, too, were still adversely criticised, and particular exception was taken to his appointing to the command of one of his privateer sloops "*John Ham*, a man notoriously known to be guilty of piracy and all manner of villany's; and particularly of a most barbarous and treacherous *murder* of five or six *Spaniards* in cold blood, whom he had invited to an entertainment of his own house." This man Ham was such a notorious pirate that it was said that he dared not show his face in the islands of Antigua, Nevis, St. Christopher or Montserrat until Parke took over the government and pardoned him.

Then the people complained of the manner in which Parke "frequently and publickly declared his implacable malice against the Island of *Antigua*," and they cited a specific instance which occurred at the house of Colonel Francis Rogers, when Parke declared that " were it not for a few friends he would send the island of Antegoa to the devil." Further, he was beard to

swear that he would clap any one in a dungeon who
was going home to complain of him to the Queen, and
would leave him to perish, adding ominously that
"there was more ways to kill a dog than one."

At night Parke would roam about the streets of
St. John's in disguise, eavesdropping and spying, and
thus bringing, as it was claimed, "his person and
authority in contempt." On these night rambles he
was generally armed with a " small ponyard, and a
case of pocket-pistoles."

The Governor characterised this accusation as
whimsical, and in his defence he throws an interesting
light on the conditions of sea ports in the West
Indies at that time. "You may easily imagine," he
wrote, "that a sea-port town in the West Indies, full
of punch-houses and taverns, cramm'd with soldiers
and privateers to be very licentious."

All these complaints were embodied in a series of
"Articles of Complaint exhibited against Daniel Parke,
Esqre.," which was eventually drawn up for despatch
to England.

Though Parke was at loggerheads with the people,
his relations with the Lords Commissioners of Trade do
not seem to have been at all strained, if one may judge
from a perusal of the despatches which passed between
him and them. In the days before cables and steam-
ship communication the representatives of the King
had far greater responsibilities than they have now,
when matters of even trivial importance are referred to
Downing Street. A regular packet service had only
been inaugurated a few years before Parke assumed the

reins of government of the Leeward Islands, and letters took anything from a month to two months to cross the Atlantic, while danger of capture by the Queen's enemies was a far more serious consideration than that of loss by stress of weather.

Up to a certain point Parke was on excellent terms with the forerunners of our Colonial Office, and it was only over a little episode in connection with the seal of the colony that any serious disagreement appears to have taken place.

Following the usual practice a new seal was prepared when Parke assumed the government of the islands and he was expected to return the old one. This he failed to do, and the matter became a subject of constant correspondence which had not been brought to a satisfactory conclusion when Parke met with his untimely end.

The following is a fair specimen of Parke's defence of his conduct with regard to the seal: "I should have sent the broken seal, if it had been in my power, tho' old Colonel Codrington and Sr. Nath. Johnson in the like case were permitted to keep it as a perquisite, the vallue of the silver is not above three or four pounds sterling. When I arrived pursuant to your order I caused the seale to be brought before the Councill and broke, the peices lay upon the table, there was a vast crowd of all sorts of people, as saylors, negroes, etc. ; when the Councill broke up, I went away and forgott it, the Deputy Secretary said he gave it to my man, he saies he put it into a table drawer, I never thought

37

of it till I went to St. Christophers, I sent about it, but the table was removed out of the house by the owner and from that day to this I never could hear what became of it; had it been possible to have procured such peices of it had it cost never so much I would have done it, but all that can be done now is to pay the value of it, the man that made the seal your Lordships Secretary gave me can inform the value of the silver, that which was broke was just such another, please to lett me know what he says 'tis worth I will order my agent to pay the money."

The sands were now running out, and the patience of the people was rapidly becoming exhausted. A sum of money was accordingly raised in the island and a Mr. W. Nevin was despatched to England to lay the grievances of the people before the Queen and Council; and the Colonial Agent—in those days each West Indian island had its agent—Mr. Richard Cary, was instructed to do all in his power to assist him in carrying out the object of his mission.

Meanwhile, an attempt was made on the life of the Governor, who was shot at by a negro as he was riding along the high road between St. John's and English Harbour, an event which was thus described by Parke in his own words : " On the 5th of September I was way laid as I came home in the evening with two gentlemen with me, and shot at from behind a hedge in a cane peice, I was shot at so near, that my horse started at the flash of the pan which saved my life, but the bullet went through the elbow up my left arme it shattered the bones, I lose soe much blood that I was two months before I was able to walk out and am still very weake my wounds are not yet closed, sevll. splinters have and are still working out, and I shall loose the use of my arme, all that my friends could doe, could not take the negroe, or him that was with him, they got them off of ye Island."

The negro who attempted to rid the island of its tyrannous governor was a man named Sandy belonging to Captain John Otto Baijers; but Parke freely accused two prominent residents, Parson Field and Colonel Thomas, of being the "contrivers" of his assassination on this occasion. A reward of 150 pieces of eight was offered for the capture of Sandy but the man was sent off the island and so escaped.

Mr. Nevin's mission proved successful. To the great satisfaction of the people he returned to Antigua with the necessary authority for the examination of witnesses to prove the articles of impeachment as well as the Governor's answer. The depositions were accordingly sworn in due form before Edward Byam, Esq., a member of Council, and Nathaniel Crump, Esq., Speaker of the House of Assembly, and instructions were issued for them to be sealed with the seal of the islands and forwarded immediately to England.

The Governor however procrastinated, and, stating that his reply was not yet ready, withheld the seal. It consequently became necessary to use another one and to send the documents to England in the care of Mr. Nevin.

Early in 1709 to the intense delight of the inhabitants Parke was recalled. At the Court of St. James, on

February 5 in that year, an Order of Council was passed instructing him to return to England to answer the complaints made against him ; and on March 25 his commission was revoked. " We have thought fit," ran the Order, " to require and Command you as we do by these Presents require and Command you, as you will answer the Contrary at Your Peril, forthwith upon the Receipt hereof to leave those Islands and return into Our presence prepar'd to make your defence before us in Councill."

The news of his recall reached him whilst he was " rejoicing with friends on 29th of May in commemoration of the Royal Family and Monarchy's being restored." " This order," he afterwards wrote, " as severe as it is, did no ways damp my mirth, but added to it, for now I shall have an opportunity to expose their perjury's and all their other villany's and prove they assasinated first my reputation."

All the same, in spite of this boast, Parke failed to obey the command ; and, remaining on the islands, he became more despotic and overbearing in his manner than ever.

He now vented his anger on the House of Assembly, whose members he treated with the utmost contumely. Ignoring their privileges, he claimed the right of appointing their clerk, and nominated a man named Hill, who was one of his worthless friends, for that position. The Assembly, on the other hand, determined that William Hinde should receive the appointment.

This led to a heated discussion, and while this state

THE ORDER IN COUNCIL SIGNED BY QUEEN ANNE
RECALLING GOVERNOR PARKE

of affairs existed Parke was writing home expressing the belief that he had got the better of the complainants. " The former Generalls," he said, " used to govern us arbitrarily as Bashas."

At about this time Codrington, his chief enemy, died, a circumstance which he reported in the following words : " Codrington (that Machivall) yt. was the author and contriver of all this villany against me is now answering for it, and a vollpony will he made takes place, so that ye most of his estate goes to those he mortally hated before he died. He was in great perplexity before he died to alter his will and according sent 6 times for one to do it, but those about him prevented the messengers going ; he lived like a wretch and dyed unlamented and had not the pleasure to hear of the order for my coming home, and they say he broke his heart, not being able to gett the better of me for ye news we had before was that I had intirely got the better and the complaint laid aside, and we were going all to be friends, till a Bristol man arriv'd at Nevis brought the news of the order then they fired their gunns and drank my Lord Sunderland's health, &c."

The quarrel between the Assembly and the Governor now became acute. The members insisted on their rights to " a negative voice " and to select their own clerk. The tactless Governor replied by twitting them in messages regarding their " chimerical privileges," and still persisted in his attempt to appoint Hill. While this acrimonious dispute was proceeding legislation was out of the question, and the affairs of the

41

islands lapsed into a state of chaos, which seems to have pleased Parke rather than otherwise, for he believed that it would lead to a compromise.

The Assembly now resorted to the last expedient of a baffled legislature and declined to vote supplies. Again and again they were in consequence dissolved. On the approach of the French fleet a new Assembly was convened, and Parke once more endeavoured to get his own way with regard to the appointment of a clerk, but still without success.

Then one day the members of the Assembly, accompanied by an unruly mob, burst into the Court House where the Governor and Council were sitting and the rabble reviled and insulted the Governor. Says French: "They call him traytor; threaten to pull him out by the beard; and a blood-thirsty man (John Kerr) officiously offers to cut his throat."

An officer, realising the danger, ordered a sergeant and a squad of grenadiers to guard the Court House door. The mob was then prevailed upon to withdraw and the Assembly was adjourned for two days.

The temper of the people was now thoroughly roused, and compromise was out of the question. Inflammatory speeches were delivered in the Market Place, and the Governor was threatened "with such a pill on Thursday as he should not digest," and with an attack "by such a force . . . as would drive him and his grenadiers to the devil!" The members of the Assembly were determined to fight for their privileges to the bitter end. That end was not far off.

The crisis came about on December 7, 1710. In the

early hours of the morning of that eventful day people began to pour into St. John's from the countryside armed with whatever weapons they could lay hands on. By daybreak it was computed that there must have been fully four hundred people under arms in the town.

Seeing the preparations which were being made Parke withdrew to his house with all the available soldiers, who numbered from forty to fifty under Colonel Newell, Lieutenant Worthington and Ensign Lyndon. Several of his more intimate friends also joined him, including Mr. Pember, Mr. Gatewood, Mr. Ayon, Mr. Beauleau, Dr. Bonnin, Mr. Rosengrave and Mr. French. He then sent Michael Ayon, the Provost Marshal, to the Market Place to read and nail up a proclamation, calling upon all persons under arms to disperse. This they resolutely declined to do, and sent the Provost Marshal back with a message telling the Governor to apply the document to a purpose which it would not be polite to mention in these pages.

Meanwhile the mob was increasing in size every minute. A proclamation was read declaring the Governor a traitor, and angry voices were raised demanding that his throat should be cut, or that he should be sent off the island in irons.

After some deliberation an Address was now conveyed to Parke by Mr. Nathaniel Crump, the Speaker of the House of Assembly, and Colonel George Gamble, a member of the Legislative Council, calling upon him to dismiss his guard and to resign the Government forthwith.

43

Whatever his other failings might have been Parke was not apparently lacking in courage. Neither threats nor the fear of death, he stoutly replied, would persuade him to quit the Government with which he had been entrusted by his Royal Mistress. If, however, the Assembly felt awed by the presence of his guard they could meet at Parham, where they would not find a single soldier. He was prepared, he said, to appoint the person whom they had chosen clerk of the Assembly and to give his assent to any laws which they might pass for the good of the island; and he would, he added, reduce his bodyguard to its normal number if six gentlemen of the highest repute would remain with him as hostages and if the mob would disperse.

Crump and Gamble having expressed their willingness to be two of the hostages then withdrew, well pleased with these concessions; and some of the malcontents on receiving their report professed themselves satisfied with the result of the interview. The more turbulent spirits were, however, in a majority. The concessions had been wrung from the Governor too late. Already the drums were beating a march, and the shouting and jeering mob was advancing towards Parke's residence.

Breaking into two parties one section of the rabble, under Captain John Piggott, approached the front of the house whilst the other, led by Captain Painter, a wealthy planter, prepared to attack it from the rear. On Church Hill a sergeant and six men had been posted with orders to hold the position against the mob, but they were at once overawed and laid down their arms.

THE FATE OF GOVERNOR PARKE

The first shot was fired by Piggott's party. Ensconced behind trees and rocks they opened a regular fusillade against the Governor's house, which Painter's men now began to attack with equal vigour from the rear.

For a time the mob was kept at bay by a field-piece which, loaded as it was with round and partridge shot, did deadly execution, but at last the house was stormed and captured. Parke had shut himself in his chamber, but it was the work of a moment only to force the door open. Headed by Captain Piggott the foremost rebels rushed into the room, and a desperate hand-to-hand struggle ensued. Piggott was killed by Parke's own hands, and for some minutes all was din and confusion. Then the Governor himself fell wounded and disabled by a shot in his thigh.

Having tasted blood the infuriated populace now wreaked a terrible vengeance on the Governor. Wounded though he was they tore off his clothes with such violence that only the wrist and neckbands of his shirt were left on him. Then they dragged him down the steps and out into the street, his head bumping from step to step. Here, if accounts are true, they continued to shout at him and revile him in a most "barbarous manner."

According to Mr. George French, who supported the Governor, Parke was now left to die, exposed to the scorching sun, and a woman who brought him some water narrowly escaped having a "sword sheath'd in her guts for her humanity, and the water is dash'd out of her hands."

The mob continued to revile and insult the Governor

even in the hour of death. "Gentlemen," he pleaded, "if you have no sense of honour left pray have some of humanity!" But his pleas were unavailing, until at last he was removed to the house near by. There after intense suffering and agony he expired. The people were revenged.

For days after St. John's was in a turmoil, and it was long before the fury of the mob was spent. After surfeiting themselves with blood, the rabble, who, according to French, had provided themselves with pillow-cases in which to carry off the plunder, looted the Governor's house and stores, helping themselves to money, plate, jewels, clothes, linen, and all that they could lay hands on.

The town continued in an uproar, and the resentment of the people against their late governor was carried to such an extreme that they even tore down his pew in the church, while several days elapsed before they allowed his mutilated corpse to be buried.

Of the Queen's forces on that day Ensign Lyndon and about fourteen soldiers were killed, and Colonel Newell, Lieutenant Worthington, and some twenty-six men wounded. Of all the personal friends who were with the Governor not one escaped unhurt. On the side of the people the losses included Captain Piggott, Mr. Thomas Young, Mr. Gervace Turton, and a man named Rayne, who were killed, and about thirty who were wounded.

After Parke's death John Yeamans assumed the government of the colony pending the arrival in

Antigua of General Walter Hamilton, who was hastily summoned from Nevis as the rightful successor of the late Governor by a deputation consisting of four members of the Legislature. Queen Anne, however, greatly wroth on hearing of the murder of her *protégé*, sent out General Walter Douglas to govern the Leeward Caribbee Islands, and instructed him to try and send home " not fewer than three nor more than six " of the ringleaders in the recent rebellion, as the affair was now described.

On reaching Antigua Douglas was forced to represent to the authorities at home that the feeling against Parke was so strong that he dared not punish those implicated in the murder. Eventually, however, John Painter, John Kerr, William Hamilton, and John King were thrown into prison at St. John's, while Mckinnon and Watkins who returned to England were also incarcerated on their arrival.

Meanwhile the Council was constantly meeting to discuss the rebellion. The partisans of Parke forwarded an Address to Queen Anne praying that the ringleaders might be punished. The detractors of the late Governor, on the other hand, pleaded with equal persistence for the release of the implicated persons.

The feeling at home at this time has been described by the "Universal History." At first, says that authority, " the people of England heard with astonishment of Parke's untimely fate ; but the public were divided in their sentiments ; some looking upon his death as an act of rebellion against the Crown, and

47

others considering it as a sacrifice to liberty. The flagrancy of the perpetuation and compassion for the man at last got the better."

"In spite, however, of "compassion for the man" the English Government after fully investigating the matter were satisfied as to Parke's misconduct and decided to issue a pardon to those who participated in the affair. On February 4, 1712, a Proclamation was issued in Antigua ordering the 20th of that month to be kept as a solemn fast in atonement for Parke's murder. Two days later Queen Anne signed a Proclamation in London pardoning all who had taken part in the rebellion, "being persuaded, that many of the offenders were drawne into that rebellion and murder by the subtle insinuations and by the influence of some of the chief advisers and promotters thereof, and not from any rancour of mind or disposition to our Government." The Proclamation provided, however, that "if any of the persons hereby meant or intended to have the benefit of this our gracious and free pardon shall presume to justifye the murder aforesaid, or shall assemble and meet together in order to obstruct justice or shall attempt like rebellious practices . . . for the future, they shall receive no benefitt . . . but be liable to prosecution."

Possibly this latter clause was the means of saving Walter Douglas' life, for the new Governor was scarcely less unpopular than his predecessor. The action which he took, very much against his own inclinations, against the ringleaders in the Parke affair had perhaps something to do with it; but he also was accused of bribery,

BUXTON GROVE, ANTIGUA

WHERE GOVERNOR PARKE BREATHED HIS LAST

of appropriating the island duties for his own use, and of other offences. The result of it all was that he was recalled to England, haled before the King's Bench, tried and sentenced to five years' imprisonment and to pay a fine of £500.

Perhaps the place of Parke's burial was not disclosed through fear lest his enemies might still further show their resentment of his misdeeds by desecrating his grave. At any rate, a careful search has failed to result in any traces of it whatever being found in the island. It has been said that Buxton Grove, a charmingly situated residence of typical West Indian appearance, with its cool looking galleries and palm-decked gardens occupies the site of a house in which the tyrannous Governor once lived, while some authorities state that Parke was shot in a building which stood where the school of Lady Mico's charity used to be and the Moravian college now is.

Tradition says that the present cathedral, with its handsome façade and twin octagonal towers, which forms such a prominent feature of the landscape as viewed from the harbour of St. John's, replaced the old militia barracks of Parke's time; but no mention is made of the latter in old maps. As to the actual spot where Parke breathed his last there is less difference of opinion, and the visitor to St. John's is usually told that the house which sheltered the mangled remains of the misguided Governor was one standing in the street to the west of the cathedral, an illustration of which is given in this volume.

Beyond this and several original documents, which

include Queen Anne's Order in Council commanding Parke to leave the islands, and the unfortunate man's will, which is given in the appendix, nothing remains in Antigua to remind the people of the misdeeds of the worst Governor who ever controlled their destinies.

CHAPTER III

THE SIEGE OF BRIMSTONE HILL

THE picturesque island of St. Christopher, in which the historic fortress known for generations as " Brimstone Hill " is situated, rises from the blue waters of the Caribbean Sea, some forty or forty-five miles to the west of Antigua, and forms with Nevis and Anguilla a presidency of our Leeward Islands colony. Discovered by Columbus in 1493 on his second voyage it was christened after his patron Saint, because—so, at least, the story goes—the shape of its rugged mountains reminded him of St. Christopher carrying our Saviour.

When the island was first settled by that great coloniser, Thomas Warner, in the year 1623 (old style), it was called Merwar's Hope (a name obviously derived from those of Ralph Merrifield, who fitted out the expedition, and of its organiser) ; but it soon reverted to its earlier and more attractive title, which was subsequently abbreviated to " St. Kitts."

To this little island belongs the proud distinction of being the Mother Colony of the British West Indies, for though Barbados was nominally taken possession of in 1605, eighteen years before St. Kitts, it was not

51

definitely settled until 1626. Warner, who, as his tomb at Middle Island Church records:

> " Bought with losse of Noble bloud Illustrious name,
>   Of A Commander Greate in Acts of Fame "

was so pleased with the appearance of St. Kitts, which apparently well deserved its original Carib name " Liamuiga," or Fertile, that; after a brief visit to England, he returned to it in 1625 with more settlers.

It is often said that Warner landed on the same day as that on which Sieur d'Esnambuc, a Norman soldier from Dieppe, disembarked with a small band of Frenchmen. John Hilton, " Storekeeper and Chief Gunner of Nevis," in a statement dated April 29, 1675, gives, however, a different story. According to him, a French castaway was already living with the Indians on the island when Warner arrived, though " de Numbec," as he calls Sieur d'Esnambuc, did not arrive until later, when Warner had become master of the whole island. According to this authority, the English welcomed the arrival of the French, feeling by no means secure against raids by the warlike Carib Indians. " A French shipp touching theire, and Capt. Warner knowing yt. those [Indians] wch. did escape would looke revenge for his owne safeguard being but weake in men, gave way to ye french to settle, and to have halfe ye island if they would settle." *

This same Hilton tells how Warner, having obtained

---

* British Museum (Egerton MS. 2395). The " History of the Island of Antigua," by Vere Langford Oliver, London, 1894, vol. i. p. xiii.

a license from the Indian King "Tegreman," settled near that dusky potentate's residence. Here he built a fort of palisades " with flanckers and loope holes for theire defence," and when the king very naturally asked what these were intended for, the settlers ingenuously replied that " it was made yt. they might look after those fowles they had about theire houses "!

Before long, as has so often happened, the existence of a common foe—in this case it was the Caribs—speedily led to a mutual understanding being arrived at between the French and English settlers. The aboriginal inhabitants assuming a menacing attitude, English and French stood shoulder to shoulder, and the Caribs, defeated in a fierce encounter, were eventually exterminated.

The colonists then devoted themselves to developing the resources of their island, the English occupying the middle part with Old Road as their capital, and the French either end with Basseterre as principal town. This, by the way, is not an isolated instance of the joint settlement of a West Indian island, for St. Martin, which now thrives partly under the flag of the Netherlands and partly under the tricolour of France, was also claimed by two settlers of different nationalities, a Dutchman and a Frenchman, who landed at the same time. A dispute arising between them, they agreed to settle it by walking round the coast in opposite directions, dividing the island by a line drawn between the point at which they started and that at which they met. The "slim" though stouter Dutchman, who was a slow walker, started off towards the more valuable end, where the salt ponds are situated, the result being that, while the Frenchman secured the larger share of the island, the richer part became Dutch.

But to return to St. Kitts. In 1629 the Spaniards under Don Frederigo de Toledo, fearing that the joint-owned island might become too powerful and prove a menace to the supremacy of Spain, drove out the French and deported many of the English colonists, some of whom, however, fled to the woods. A few plucky French settlers also remained, and with their assistance d'Esnambuc succeeded in re-establishing the colony. By the Peace of Breda in 1667 the English had their part of the island restored to them; but twenty-two years later they were again expelled. In 1689 Sir Timothy Thornhill, Major-General of the Militia in Barbados, with a force of 700 men which he had raised there, landed on June 21 at the Salt Ponds on that curiously shaped spit of land which stretches towards Nevis. Marching over the hill, known ever since as Timothy Hill, he took the French completely by surprise, and advancing on the town of Basseterre he successfully plundered it.

It was at this period that the value of Brimstone Hill as a strategic base was first properly appreciated and from the initial attack upon it until its final evacuation the English frequently withdrew to it, for the French returned to their portion of the island after the Treaty of Ryswick in 1697.

England again became sole mistress of St. Kitts in 1702, and though the island was captured by the French early in 1782, it was restored to us by the

Treaty of Versailles which followed Rodney's decisive victory over de Grasse.

Rising in solitary grandeur on the sea-shore about ten miles from Basseterre, Brimstone Hill forms a striking landmark. Geologists state that it consists of a mass of limestone overlying volcanic rock. To the layman it certainly looks as if at some remote period it had been ejected from the craters of the rugged mountains which form the backbone of the island, and culminate in the majestic and awe-inspiring peak, Mount Misery, towering to a height of 3711 feet. Viewed from land or sea, the battlements with which the hill is crowned give it the appearance of a frowning fortress; but its glories have long since departed, and it stands now bereft of its garrison, deserted and dismantled, a proud relic of the past. Though British still, the Union Jack has ceased to float over its citadel, and its batteries no longer ring with martial sounds.

In 1674 Sir William Stapleton, Captain-General of the Leeward Islands, who described it as a " pitiful place," did not contest the claim of the French to an interest in the hill, which was then used as a source of supply of the commodity which gave it its name. As already stated, it was not until 1690 that the value of this position for defence purposes was first recognised. It was in that year, during the governorship of Codrington, the father of the pious founder of the college in Barbados, which bears his name, that guns were first hauled up its steep slopes under the directions of Sir Timothy Thornhill. The task was a difficult one, and we read that Codrington doubted if he could have accomplished it "but for our trusty regiment of sailors," which reminds us that our "handymen" were as resourceful then as they are now in cases of emergency. Six pieces of cannon were planted on the hill, and these proved sufficient to compel the French to evacuate a great fort situated immediately below, a feat which was celebrated by hoisting the English flag while the troops "drank their Majesties' healths to a round of all the guns in the fort, which was answered by the frigates and three volleys of the whole army." In 1699 the hill was rendered practically inaccessible by heavy guns mounted in the topmost works. It had, even at that early date, cisterns to hold water and was "planted with Indian provision (presumably cassava) fit to maintain a sufficient number of men to keep it six months."

In 1706, during the régime of the notorious Governor Parke, the fort was practically destroyed through the magazine being struck by lightning. In a letter to the Lords Commissioners of Trade and Plantations, dated October 5, in that year Parke wrote "The lightning sett fire to our magazine on Brimstone Hill and blew up all the powder, and threw down one bastion of the Fort, killed a Lieutenant and several men, the Island must be at great charge to maintain the soldiers and new build that part of the Fort that is destroyed; God help us, we are the only unhappy people of the Queen's Dominions." Lightning conductors were not invented until 1752, and it is not surprising to learn that the hill was again struck in 1731, when 150 barrels of gunpowder were destroyed upon it.

THE SIEGE OF BRIMSTONE HILL

Before his untimely end, which is dealt with in another chapter, Parke rebuilt the fort, and in 1716 Brimstone Hill, which until that year had apparently only been leased, was purchased by the Government of St. Kitts from the owner, Governor William Matthew, for the sum of £500 and a parcel of land in another part of the island. As the hill was entailed, an Act was passed by the Legislature to enable the sale to be effected. The terms of it were as follows:

"St. Kitts, *November*, 1716.

"An Act to enable William Matthew, an infant under 21, to convey a parcel of land in St. Kitts called Brimstone Hill, and Vest the inheritance thereof in His Majesty for the Fortification, and for settling other land on William Matthew and his heirs, in lieu and for the payment of £500 to the Hon. William Matthew his Father in consideration of the same. Whereas the Hon. Wm. Matthew, Esq., Lt.-General of H.M.'s Leeward and Caribbee Is: and Lt.-Governor of St. Kitts is seized of a parcel of land called Brimstone Hill containing in circumference one mile—as tenant by Curtesie of England by virtue of his marriage with Anne Matthew his late Wife (sole daughter and heir of Thos. Hill, Esq., of St. Kitts, dec:) and whereas William Matthew had by her William Matthew his only son, who is lawfully entitled to the reversion and inheritance in fee simple after the death of his Father, being only son and heir of Anne Matthew, and whereas the said land is suited from its situation to defend the Fort of Charles Fort,

57

and Lt.-Governor Matthew has agreed for £500 cur: to lease all demands of rent since the death of Thomas Hill for 19 years past and to settle other lands of greater value on his son in lieu and his son is now an infant, etc., etc., William Matthew agrees to confirm to his son when of age the reversion of 23 acres in the Parish of St. Thomas Middle Island lately purchased by Michael Lambert, Esq.

"JOHN HART,
"*Deputy Clerk of Council.*"

William Matthew did not do so badly, for the lands which were conveyed to him in exchange for the hill were among the finest in the island. They are still in the possession of the family of Buckley Matthew.

In 1740 the fort was " planted with 49 pieces of cannon," and it contained " a magazine supplyed with 18,000 pounds of powder, 800 firelocks, 600 bayonets and other military stores." *

Though the massive works, the ruins of which are now seen, were not completed until twelve years after the siege, Brimstone Hill was considered one of the strongest positions in the West India Islands when the memorable attack was made upon it by the French under de Bouillé in 1782. The elaborate fortifications were built by slave labour, each estate's proprietor being compelled to furnish one out of every eighty slaves which he possessed as his contribution towards their erection.

During the American War, the people of St. Kitts

* "The Gentleman's Magazine," vol. x., 1740, p. 241.

were, to put it mildly, by no means so loyal as they now are. It is, indeed, an admitted fact that they sympathised more or less openly with the revolted colonists, and enriched themselves by carrying on a contraband trade in munitions of war with the Dutch island of St. Eustatius—now generally called Statia for short— which, being a free port, became famous as the principal entrepôt of the West Indies.

Huge warehouses, the ruins of which can still be seen, were erected on the seashore, and the merchants prospered exceedingly until February 13, 1781, when Rodney seized this Dutch island, together with two hundred vessels of various nationalities, and war supplies and merchandise to the value of several million pounds. This enraged the good merchants of St. Kitts, who, not without success, brought actions against Rodney for the recovery of their goods. Incidentally it may be remarked in this connection that many even now believe that much treasure still lies buried in St. Eustatius, and it is said that, some few years ago, a landowner there who was digging a hole for the reception of a gatepost, struck gold to the value of three hundred pounds sterling six inches below the surface.

The people of St. Kitts remained disaffected until the end of the war, and but for this regrettable fact it is doubtful if Brimstone Hill would have yielded to the assault of de Bouillé in the operations which will now be described.

It had been the intention of this gallant Marquis, as he can truthfully be called, to reduce Barbados : but the fleet under de Grasse, upon whose support he was depending, was driven so far to leeward by adverse winds that a change of plan became necessary, and on January 11, 1782, he landed 8000 men on St. Kitts, having decided to devote his attention to that island instead of the more easterly colony.

The first intimation of the approach of the enemy was received by Governor Shirley on January 9. It is recorded in the journal of the siege, which was carefully kept day by day, that at about 4 p.m. on that day, he " received a dispatch from Mr. Herbert, President of Nevis, informing him that a large fleet, consisting of about forty sail, twenty-four of which were large ships and the rest sloops and schooners had appeared in sight of that Island. In consequence whereof an alarm was directed to be forthwith fired at Basseterre, and orders issued that all matrosses and their officers together with part of the militia, should immediately repair to the several batteries and be ready to act upon any emergency."

As to following day : " The weather being very hazy, the fleet was not distinctly perceived till the afternoon, when upwards of forty sail were seen standing for St. Christopher's ; whereupon the Russel man of war then under sail, bore away and stood to the southward ; and at the same time Genl. Shirley received a letter from Mr. White, deputy lieutenant Governor of Monserrat, acquainting him that the said fleet, consisting of about 19 or 20 sail of the line, a few frigates and a considerable number of small vessels had passed by that Island, and seemed to be making the Island of St. Christopher."

THE SIEGE OF BRIMSTONE HILL

"At daybreak," on Friday, January 11, "the enemy's fleet was discovered a little to the southward of Nevis Point, bearing directly down for St. Christopher's, consisting of about 28 sail of the line and a number of small craft. The militia being assembled about 8 o'clock a.m. by orders of the preceding night, General Shirley appeared on their parade and led about 350 of them to join the King's troops upon Brimstone Hill and upon our march we were very much annoyed by a detachment of three line of battle ships and four frigates from the Enemy's fleet that were sent to intercept a number of merchant ships that were endeavouring to escape, and by a well-directed fire from our line of batteries the enemy were foiled in their attempt and most of the merchantmen got shelter under the guns of Brimstone Hill and Fort Charles. The same detachment then made the best of their way back in order to rejoin the rest of the fleet which had come to an anchor in the Road of Basseterre, and a number of the enemy's troops was in the afternoon landed near the town and took possession of the batteries there. This evening all the outposts were called in and 71 seamen joined the garrison."

In the endeavour to disembark the powerful artillery originally destined for the reduction of Barbados, the ship which contained the heaviest and most effective part of it, "together with a prodigious quantity of shells, balls and ordnance stores," had struck the rocks and sunk.

On the approach of the French, the British garrison, which did not exceed 600 effective men under General

Fraser, at once retired to Brimstone Hill, " on which fortifications had only recently been erected and were still far from being complete." Here they were joined soon after by the local militia under Governor Shirley, who " carried the seal of the Leeward Islands with him," a circumstance which led to President John Jarvis complaining to Lord St. Germain that " whilst Mr. Shirley is confined with the seals at Brimstone Hill in St. Christopher's, no public act of any of the islands can be passed into Law." Jarvis added that the " military gentlemen " said " that the fort on Brimstone Hill " could " not be undermined but by the tedious operation of drilling a solid rock."

The height of Brimstone Hill, coupled with the fact that it had no proper roads, rendered it, at that time, almost inaccessible, and it was considered quite one of the strongest posts in the West India Islands. It was believed that a garrison of 2000 men could have rendered it impregnable as long as provisions lasted : but the number of troops available was not sufficient for a long siege. Moreover, owing to the disaffection of the colonists, who would give the soldiers no assistance, eight brass twenty-four pounders, 6000 balls of the same calibre, two brass 13-inch mortars and 1500 shells for the supply of the fortress, could not be carried up, but were found at the foot of the hill by the enemy, to whom they " proved a most seasonable and necessary supply in the prosecution of the siege." This unfortunate circumstance, but for the occurrence of which the garrison would probably, in Sir Samuel Hood's opinion, not have been reduced, together with the fact that the

British were " totally destitute of entrenching tools,"
rendered the position of General Fraser extremely
difficult. The approach to the hill was so steep that it
did not require much artificial aid to enable a very few
men to repel any sudden assault; but the works and
buildings at the top were, unfortunately, ill capable at
that time of withstanding the batteries of heavy cannon
and mortars, which the undisturbed possession of the
adjoining country, and the weakness of the garrison,
enabled the enemy to establish at the most convenient
distances, and in the most advantageous positions.

The French forces were drawn from the regiments of
Armagnac, Champagne, Auxerre, Agène, Vienne and
Touraine and included much artillery. Having landed
his men on January 11 de Bouillé began to advance
upon the hill under cover of darkness at 10 o'clock p.m.,
and that night some of his advance parties fired on the
English sentries. On the next day the English could,
from their commanding position, see his reconnoitring
parties being " very much molested by the negroes of
the neighbouring estates . . . Several prisoners, among
whom was the Adjutant of the Viennois Regiment,
were brought into the garrison by them; and so alert
were those negroes that a servant of the Marquis de
Bouillé was actually taken prisoner and the Marquis
himself narrowly escaped; in consequence whereof the
enemy advanced a corps under the fire of the garrison,
and set in flames a plantation belonging to a Mr. Wells,
and the Marquis de Bouillé sent in a flag to remonstrate
against the conduct of the negroes, threatening that
unless they should be restrained he would immediately

lay waste the country. The servant was released and the Adjutant was discharged on parole."

On Sunday, the 13th, the negroes continued to harass the French. They killed a French officer and brought in another belonging to an artillery regiment as a prisoner. Generals Shirley and Fraser, however, in order to convince de Bouillé of their disapproval of such conduct sent an officer of the 15th Regiment with a flag of truce to hand over the French prisoner, for which generous act they received the thanks of the Marquis.

The loss of the heaviest part of the French artillery and the subsequent capture by the British, under Sir Samuel Hood (afterwards Viscount Hood), of the frigate which was bringing a fresh supply from Martinique augured well for the garrison, but the enemy, nothing daunted, successfully raised many of their guns and were also fortunate enough to receive reinforcements from Martinique.

De Bouillé went about his work in a thoroughly business-like manner, and left nothing to chance. Indeed, he " found the adventure attended with so much difficulty that he carried on his approaches and opened trenches under all the formalities of the most regular siege." His headquarters were established at Sandy Point, a small town at the foot of the hill, to which the garrison in the fortress soon set fire, playing upon it so effectively with their heavy cannon and mortars that the French could not extinguish the flames until it was totally consumed. A quantity of powder, for which there was no room in the magazines

ATTAQUE DE BRIMSTOMHILL.

THE SIEGE OF BRIMSTONE HILL

From an engraving by M. N. Ponce after the painting by M. le Paon

on the hill, had been left in the King's Stores close to the English lines, and on the 14th the picquets seeing the enemy approaching set fire to it. The precaution had been taken of spreading the powder out lest the works and cisterns should be damaged, and so there was no serious explosion; but some of the buildings and stores caught fire, including provisions and all the clothing of the 15th Regiment, the carriages of eight 24-pounders which had already been spiked, the beds of two 13-inch mortars, one 10-inch mortar and four 8-inch mortars.

The events of the succeeding days are best described by Governor Shirley's journal, from which some idea of the rigours of the siege may be gathered:

"Wednesday, Jan. 16. Apprehending that part of the enemy were still lodged in the back part of the town of Sandy Point, the cannonade was repeated for a short time and parties were employed in bringing up mortars that had been spiked from the foot of the Hill. Two deserters from the Irish Brigade came in this morning and reported that the French army consisted of about eight thousand men, and that a ship lately sunk off Sandy Point was a store ship containing ordnance, stores and ammunition for the field, particularly their bombs, the loss of which had occasioned their being so tardy in their operations. About 11 o'clock at night another deserter came in and the enemy being hard at work about the environs, the garrison were ordered to their alarm posts where they remained till day.

"Thursday, Jan. 17. A working party of seamen

and negroes were employed in placing the mortars and forming platforms for them. We discovered that the enemy had begun to break ground at Summersal's Estate* on Sandy-point side, distant about 700 yards, whereupon a firing was kept up in order to interrupt them and was repeated frequently during the night.

"Friday, Jan. 18. At daybreak it was perceived that the enemy had thrown up several intrenchments on Summersal's and Rawlins'† Estates distant about 700 yards each and during the day a constant fire was maintained in order to impede them.

"Saturday, Jan. 19. This day the enemy opened a battery of seven mortars from Rawlins' Estate and bombarded the garrison very briskly, which was returned by a warm cannonade from us; nevertheless the enemy continued their fire during the night.

"Sunday, Jan. 20. Seven mortars continued to play upon the garrison, which was returned by us with such good effect that the enemy were obliged to cease their fire from Rawlins' battery at 5 o'clock p.m.

"Monday, Jan. 21. No fire was received from the enemy until about 12 o'clock at noon, when a battery of three mortars or howitzers was opened at Wells'

---

* Summersal's Estate, which is still identified by the same name, was the property of Stafford Somersall, Esq. The Somersall family eventually received an indemnity of some thousands of pounds for the damage done to the property by the French.

† Rawlins' Estate belonged to Stedman Rawlins, Esq.

Estate from whence a quick fire was kept up by the enemy and returned from the garrison by a well-directed cannonade. The firing ceased on both sides about five o'clock in the afternoon.

"Tuesday, Jan. 22. The firing about 4 o'clock in the morning was renewed from the batteries at Rawlins' and Wells' Estates and maintained with much impetuosity till about 10 o'clock p.m. when it began to slacken and about 6 o'clock it entirely ceased. This day we discovered that the enemy had broke ground at Burke's in the rear of Summersal's Estate.

"Wednesday, Jan. 23. Very little firing on either side during the night, but at 5 o'clock in the morning it was renewed on both sides and about ten in the morning the enemy's magazine at the battery on Rawlins' Estate was blown up by a shell from one of our Royal mortars, whereby the enemy there was put in confusion, the houses and stores totally destroyed and we have reason to conclude that the enemy sustained a considerable loss both in men and ammunition. A new battery, consisting of 6 or 7 mortars, was opened upon us this morning from Summersal's Estate, distant about 700 yards, from whence the fire at times was very warm, but from Rawlins' and Wells' batteries we received very little fire. A smart cannonade was kept up from the garrison in order to slacken the enemy's fire at Summersal's and impede them in repairing their works at Rawlins' and Wells'."

On January 24 the garrison were cheered by the

welcome arrival of Sir Samuel Hood with his fleet of twenty-two ships of the line from Barbados. General Shirley in his journal records: " A number of signals being made by the enemy's fleet during the night and perceiving them in great motion in the morning we judged that the British fleet was approaching and about 8 o'clock we discovered one of our advanced frigates and soon after the squadron under the command of Sir Samuel Hood, consisting of 22 sail of the line, besides frigates, whereupon the French fleet left Basseterre Road and put to sea. During this day we received a brisk fire from the enemy's works."

Hood brought with him the 69th Regiment (now the 2nd battalion Welsh Regiment) from Barbados, besides General Prescott and the 28th Regiment (now the Gloucestershire) and two companies of the 13th (the Somerset Light Infantry) which he had picked up at Antigua. His intention had been to attack de Grasse, whose fleet lay off Basseterre at daybreak on the 24th, but a collision between the *Alfred* and the *Nymphe* necessitated a change of plan and the fleet lay to for a day, during which the *Espien*, a French cutter, loaded with stores for the siege and commanded by a Knight of Malta, was captured. At 1 p.m. on the 24th Hood rounded the south end of Nevis, and enticing de Grasse with his twenty-four ships of the line and two fifties out to sea, he successfully captured the anchorage, a brilliant manœuvre, which was watched by crowds of excited onlookers from the slopes of Nevis. He failed, however,

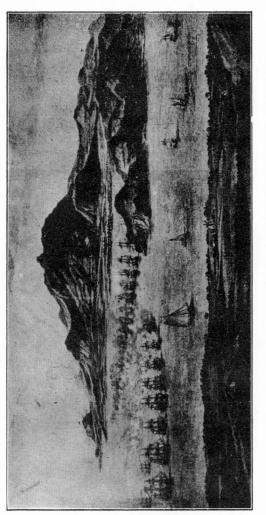

HOOD'S CAPTURE OF THE ANCHORAGE OF BASSETERRE FROM DE GRASSE
ON JANUARY 24, 1782

materially to relieve the situation, for the inhabitants of St. Kitts, though now not actually hostile, continued to observe a strict neutrality.

On gaining the anchorage, Hood and Prescott sent Lieut. Potter of the 15th Regiment to the garrison to ascertain what assistance was required. Governor Shirley placed too great reliance on the strength of the position and only requested that he might be furnished with an able naval officer and a few seamen "for the better management of this artillery." For the rest, he said that, as Prescott had taken the trouble to come with his troops to his assistance, he would be glad of the honour of seeing him, but he was in no want of him or his troops.

To return to Governor Shirley's journal:

"Friday, January 25. . . . At daybreak we perceived both fleets off Nevis Point, the British to windward of the French. The fleets being employed in manœuvring during the morning, about two o'clock the English fleet forming a Line a head stretched in for Basseterre and brought the enemy to an action, which continued to the close of the day, during which time numbers of store ships and transports put out of Basseterre and stood away for St. Eustatius. After the action the English fleet came to an anchor in Basseterre Road and the French fleet stood out to sea. On this day about noon a 5-gun Battery at Binkes' Estate, distant about 1050 yards, opened upon us. During the night Mr. Geir of the 28th Regiment made his way good to the garrison with a message from General Prescott.

"Saturday, Jan. 26. We observed the French fleet to the southward of Nevis standing in for Basseterre Road, where they attacked the British fleet : at the same time the enemy began an incessant fire upon the garrison with their mortars and cannon and continued it till midnight. This day the enemy's fire destroyed the building wherein our whole stock of rum was deposited, and a store which contained a considerable quantity of provisions and arms, and every building on the Hill except two small rooms."

General Fraser gives the additional information that on this day the enemy began to erect a battery to command Fig Tree Bay, by Mr. Brotherson's Crab Hill Works.

On Sunday, January 27, and the two following days a brisk fire was maintained by both sides without any material result.

Prescott landed on the following day and established a post on a hill just to the east of Frigate Bay, but he was driven back in a smart skirmish with the Irish Brigade who were assisting the French under M. de Flechin, losing forty killed and wounded. De Bouillé hastened to follow up the attack, but he found Prescott so advantageously posted near the sea that he did not venture to attack him, but returned to the siege.

On January 30 de Bouillé invited the garrison to surrender, pointing out the hopelessness of their position ; but Governor Shirley replied : "I am very much obliged to your Excellency for the information contained in your letter of this date ; but must inform you that this garrison is in good order, the troops in high spirits, and that we are determined to maintain this post to the last extremity."

On January 31 an incessant fire was maintained, but "nothing worth remarking occurred," though during the night several of the militia deserted, bringing the total number of deserters to forty-three. For a whole week a hot fire was kept up, but little damage was done excepting on February 6, when the enemy set fire to two stores at the foot of the hill which had escaped the fire of January 14. They were also seen breaking ground below Otley's house about nine hundred yards distant on Sandy Point side, while General Fraser adds that they had mounted guns by Brotherson's sugar-works.

All communication with the hill was now completely cut off, and the French showed the utmost vigilance. Captain Curgenven and Lieutenant Hare with thirty men in two boats endeavoured to reach the shore, but though their oars were muffled and every precaution was taken, they were received with volley after volley of musketry and were compelled to return. Two nights later a single man in a canoe tried to land, and on the same evening, Lieutenant Fahie, of the *Russel*—who afterwards became Admiral Sir William Fahie—succeeded in effecting a landing at Red Flag Bay, at the north of the island. Being a creole of St. Kitts, Fahie knew every accessible path ; but after two nights, he too had to give up his attempt to reach the fortress. On February 8 Curgenven, with Captain Bourne and

71

Fahie, made another desperate effort to reach General Fraser, but all three were made prisoners. Although he had gained such a brilliant victory over de Grasse, Hood was thus practically helpless, and he had the mortification of understanding the signals of distress which, in spite of Governor Shirley's optimism, General Fraser was compelled to show, without being able to render him any assistance.

The situation was now becoming a serious one for the defenders, as Governor Shirley's journal shows:

" Monday, February 11. We discovered that the enemy had again broken ground on Wells' Estate and were busily employed in dragging cannon to that quarter : and also that they had opened a battery of 4 guns near the well at the foot of the Hill, against the north-west front, from whence they very much annoyed the garrison on the highest parts. Twenty-three pieces of cannon and all their [mortars were this day incessantly played upon the Hill, whereby the breaches already made were greatly widened and the garrison became much reduced by killed and wounded."

The hill was now completely surrounded with batteries which were constantly, night and day, cannonading and bombarding the garrison. Trenches were successively opened on Summersal's, Rawlins', Wells', and Otley's Estates ; and, during the greater part of the last three weeks of the siege, all the force and effect of twenty-three pieces of heavy cannon, and of twenty-four large mortars were directed against a spot of ground which did not exceed 200 yards in diameter. It is said that the French

took their guns to the summit of a yet higher hill
to the north-east, which was only accessible from the
other side of the island, and from that position they
could, of course, be used with deadly effect.

All the houses on the summit of the hill were consumed by fire or blown to pieces early in the operations.
The defensive works were everywhere crumbling. To
aggravate matters, numbers of the militia had deserted
and the remainder, fearing that they would lose their
estates if they resisted any further, presented a petition
to Governor Shirley urging him to surrender. The
works on one side were at last so knocked to pieces that
an entire and perfect breach was formed and nearly all
the guns were dismounted or disabled. There were,
moreover, not more than five hundred men left who
were in a fit state for duty. On the evening of February 12 the position became untenable and, yielding
to the petition of the militia, Shirley offered to
capitulate.

Captain Robinson was accordingly sent from the
garrison to M. St. Simon, one of the French generals,
with a letter proposing a cessation of hostilities ; and,
at the same time, another officer was despatched on a
similar errand to de Bouillé, whom he found unable to
disguise his eagerness to gain possession of the hill.
At 10 o'clock the French general himself ascended the
hill, terms of capitulation were speedily agreed upon,
and the memorable siege which had lasted four weeks
and four days was at an end.

The events of the final day of the siege are thus
described by Governor Shirley:

"Tuesday, February 12. This day, on the north-west front was an entire breach and all the guns disabled. In the curtain were two very large breaches; the whole parapet was destroyed, and only one 8-inch howitzer remained serviceable. In the left flank all the guns were disabled and in the left face was a practicable breach of forty feet. This day one of our frigates appearing off Basseterre, we repeated our signals shewing the fleet the situation of our garrison. In the evening, having received a memorial from the militia in garrison, of which the paper No. 3 is a copy, it was judged proper to call upon the engineer and the commanding officer of the Artillery for their reports of the state of the defences, whereof No. 4 and 5 are copies, and upon the principal officers of the garrison for their opinion of the prospect of success which our numbers afforded us, in resisting an assault, which we had strong reason to expect would be attempted by the enemy. Governed by the result of these enquiries we were of opinion that it was expedient for the King's Service to beat a parley, and offer to capitulate for the surrender of the garrison upon terms honourable to his Majesty's arms and advantageous to the Colony."

The following is the report submitted by Lieutenant Hamilton of the Royal Artillery on the state of the works :—

"Upon our opening the batteries on the lower works, on the first appearance of the enemy, there was two twenty four pounders, four twelve pounders, two nine pounders and one eight inch howitzer mounted. The carriages were then in a very ruinous state and consequently very unfit for constant firings. The progress of the enemy, since they have opened their gun batteries, has been so heavy and rapid in the destruction of these works that the eight inch howitzer only remains serviceable, and from the present ruinous and exposed state of the whole front can only be brought into action in the night, when it is supposed that the enemy's fire has abated and they are making approach to assault. The other pieces of ordnance mentioned are mostly disabled and the whole of the carriages totally so. Upon the new battery to the eastward there was originally four brass twenty four pounders and one twelve pounder mounted. The four brass guns are still serviceable but the carriages are still disabled, two of them entirely so, and the other two from repeated firing are so much shattered that these two guns will probably in a day or so be dismounted. The twelve pounders, both gun and carriage, are disabled.

"The guns and carriages in the different parts of the garrison are in the worst state and are absolutely insufficient to prevent the approaches of the enemy.

> "GEORGE LEWIS HAMILTON.
> 1st Lieut. Commanding a
> Detachment of R.A.

" Names of Officers present :
1st Lieut. George Lewis Hamilton.
Surgeon John Rollo.

" *Captains.* William Kingsmill, Gustavus Nicolls, Thomas Wallace, Benjamin Bloomfield, Joseph Buckeridge, William Oliver Grace.

" *Lieuts.* Robert Mein, James Macgregor, George Bloomfield, Edward Pemberton, Joseph Mackay, J. Campbell, A. Stewart, Francis Manooch.

" *Ensigns.* Christr. Morshead, Allan Maclean, Dugald Stewart."

The French showed themselves magnanimous in the hour of victory, and every condition claimed, whether in favour of the garrison or of the island, was agreed to.* The British troops were allowed all the honours of war in the fullest sense. The Governor, the Commander of the troops, the regular officers and soldiers, the officers and privates of militia, marched through the breach in the fort with drums beating and colours flying, dragging with them a mortar, two field pieces and carrying ten rounds of ammunition each, with arms and baggage. All with the exception of the officers laid down their arms at a place appointed. The regular troops were considered prisoners of war, and were sent to England in " safe and good vessels," furnished with provisions for the voyage ; but they were forbidden to serve against the King of France until exchanged. The officers were permitted to reside in any of the islands on parole. The English inhabitants were obliged to take oaths of fidelity to the King of France, and they were pledged to observe an exact

* The Articles of Capitulation are given in the Appendix.

neutrality, on the understanding that they would not be compelled to take up arms against his Britannic Majesty or any other power. Until peace was declared, they were to enjoy their own laws, customs and ordinances. The inhabitants were to be supported in the possession of their estates and properties, and in their privileges, rights, titles, honours and exemptions, and in the possession of their religion, and their ministers in the enjoyment of their livings. The merchants were to enjoy all the privileges of commerce granted to the subjects of King Louis XVI. throughout all the extent of his dominions. Out of respect to their courage and determined conduct, General Shirley and General Fraser were not considered prisoners of war, and as a mark of particular esteem for those brave officers, General Shirley was permitted to return to his Government in Antigua, while General Fraser was allowed to continue in the service of his country.

On February 13 Captain Robinson of the 15th Regiment brought the news of the surrender of the hill to General Prescott, and on the following night Hood, who was bitterly disappointed, silently left Basseterre anchorage, which he had so skilfully captured less than a month before, with his fleet at 11 o'clock at night. Cables were cut and lights were left attached to buoys, de Grasse who had gone to Nevis to victual his ship being again outwitted.

The triumph of the French was, however, short-lived, and St. Kitts was restored to England by the Treaty of Versailles in 1783, which followed the brilliant and decisive victory gained by Rodney over

77

de Grasse in the Battle of the Saints off Dominica on the glorious 12th April, 1782.

Mention has already been made of the attitude of the colonists during the struggle which was terminated by that great victory, and it is noteworthy that on March 11, 1784, some gentlemen in London interested in the West India Islands which had been taken by the French voted an address of thanks and a piece of plate to de Bouillé as a public testimony of their " veneration and esteem" and of the "humanity, justice, and generosity so exemplarily displayed by him in his several conquests and chief command " of the conquered islands.

In the years which immediately succeeded this memorable siege, the fortifications were greatly strengthened ; but no shot was ever again fired from them in anger. The fighting days of this Gibraltar of the West Indies, as it has—in deference to its appearance only—appropriately been called, were ended. The fortress was, however, kept in a high state of efficiency, and one or more regiments were always stationed there. Nelson, in one of his letters to Mrs. Nisbet, refers to an engagement to dine upon the hill, which with several other prospective entertainments he viewed as involving " a good deal of fag." This was in 1787, when Prince William Henry—afterwards Duke of Clarence and King William IV. was being fêted during his stay on the Leeward Islands station in the *Pegasus* ; and we may be certain that his Royal Highness more than once forgathered with the officers of the garrison in the once palatial mess-room which is now reduced to

78

FORT GEORGE, AT THE SUMMIT

THE RUINS OF THE OFFICERS' QUARTERS

BRIMSTONE HILL, ST. KITTS

a ruin. The garrison was not finally withdrawn from Brimstone Hill until 1857. In that year the guns were dismounted and removed, and the wooden buildings and stores were sold or otherwise disposed of by the Colonial Government, to which the hill was transferred by the War Office. Brimstone Hill was then leased to an adjoining landowner for a term of years, during which many acts of vandalism were committed, the hardwood doors and window-frames being ruthlessly torn from the masonry and removed, and the bush allowed to obliterate all traces of many of the interesting buildings. On the expiration of the lease in 1901 the local Government again resumed possession, but it was not until 1902 that it was decided to preserve the ruins as a historic monument. At the instance of Mr. Charles T. Cox, C.M.G. (who is, by the way, the great grandson of Lieutenant Fahie mentioned above), the Administrator, a lime burning industry was started, and arrangements were made at the request of Sir Gerald Strickland, the then Governor of the Leeward Islands, by the Legislature for the provision of a sufficient sum of money annually to clear the fortifications from undergrowth, and to repair by degrees the damaged portions of the masonry. So well has the work been carried out since then under the guidance of the Hon. L. M. Kortright, the Superintendent of Public Works, that it is now possible to recognise quite clearly the position of the various barracks and fortifications, though few traces of the earlier works now remain. A winding road leads to the summit of the hill, and though all woodwork has

79

long since been destroyed and only the masonry is left, the various batteries and bastions, the barracks and officers' quarters can all be clearly recognised, while the immense tanks and catchment basins—for the garrison was entirely dependent on a heaven-sent water supply—are a never ending source of wonderment. Of pathetic interest is the little cemetery with its weather-worn tombstones to the memory of non-commissioned officers who died on the hill, and of surprising charm is the loggia of the officers' quarters. A flight of one hundred and fourteen steps leads to the parade ground at the base of that part of the hill on the summit of which stand the massive ruins of Fort George, the proud citadel of the fortress.

The parade ground no longer resounds with the tramp of feet, the bugle is not heard any more, and the quiet of the hill is now only disturbed by the merry laughter of picnic parties for which it is a favoured spot. If the fortifications, the remains of which are now shown, had been completed before 1782 it is inconceivable that the fortress would have fallen. Indeed, even battered as they were on February 12, the result of the siege would probably have been very different if the garrison had been able to hold out for ten days longer; for Sir Samuel Hood, in his despatches, said that he was very confident that Count de Grasse—who had remained in the neighbourhood of St. Kitts during the entire period of the siege—was weary of his situation; and, as the Marquis de Bouillé was destroying every fort and magazine at Basseterre, Hood was satisfied that the French despaired of success. But, added Hood : " I am far from meaning in the most distant manner to suggest that the garrison could have held out a single day longer, as I am told the works and buildings were a heap of ruins, and that no further defence could be made with the least probable prospect of success."

CHAPTER IV

THE BATTLE OF THE SAINTS

THE story of Rodney's brilliant victory over de Grasse in the action which has been handed down to history as the "Battle of the Saints" has been often told, and the writer cannot claim to be in a position to throw any new light upon that glorious event. It would, however, savour almost of heresy to omit from a volume of West Indian tales an account of the battle which resulted in the triumph of our sailors on the memorable April 12, 1782.

The opening months of that year found the fortunes of England at a deplorably low ebb. On all sides she was beset by her enemies. In October, 1781, Yorktown had fallen, Lord Cornwallis having surrendered with upwards of 6000 men to Generals Washington and Rochambeau with an allied army of 21,000 men. While a death-blow was thus given to all pretensions of British sovereignty over the revolted American colonies, the fate of our West Indian possessions hung in the balance. Francis Joseph Paul de Tilly, Count de Grasse, the French admiral who through the skilful disposition of his fleet had contributed in no small measure to the success

82

of American arms, by cutting off the British troops from their supplies and by preventing their retreat by water, had sailed down the islands with the intention of sweeping the British from the West Indies.

His efforts in this direction were so far successful that within a very short space of time Jamaica, Barbados and Antigua alone remained to us of our old West Indian colonies, while St. Lucia was the only island among our more recent possessions over which the Union flag still floated.

England was at this time not only at war with France and America, but also with Spain and Holland, while the attitude of the other Powers towards her, though ostensibly neutral, was one of ill-disguised hostility owing to the right which we claimed, and exercised, of searching vessels at sea. In the Mediterranean, Elliot, afterwards Lord Heathfield, was being closely besieged by France and Spain at Gibraltar, and to make matters worse Ireland was giving trouble at home.

It was while England's political relations with foreign Powers were in this unsettled state that Sir George Brydges Rodney was sent out to the West Indies. That gallant admiral had only returned from the Caribbean, where he had aroused the anger of the colonists by seizing the island of St. Eustatius and suppressing the illicit trade which was being conducted there, in the preceding year. Lord Sandwich, who was in charge of the Admiralty, now said to him: " The fate of this Empire is in your hands, and I have no wish that it should be in any other."

Rodney accordingly set sail from Torbay on January 16,

1782, in his flagship the *Formidable*, 90 guns, with eleven
sail of the line, and reached Carlisle Bay, Barbados, on
February 19. There he was joined a few days later by
Sir Samuel Hood fresh from his success over de Grasse
in the Basseterre Roads, St. Kitts—a success which did
not, however, prevent the capitulation of the garrison
which had been besieged in the fortress of Brimstone
Hill, and the surrender of the island to the magnanimous
Marquis de Bouillé.

Hearing, on arrival at Barbados, that de Grasse was
lying at Fort Royal Bay, Martinique, actively com-
pleting his arrangements for a contemplated descent on
Jamaica, Rodney proceeded without delay to St. Lucia,
which he had long regarded as an ideal naval base.
Indeed, it was in consequence of his representations that
that island was captured from the French in 1778, when
Count d'Estaing was defeated by a powerful body of
English troops which were landed at Grand Cul de
Sac Bay.

Near the northernmost point of St. Lucia there is a
spacious bay over which a tiny island about a mile and
a half long and barely three-quarters of a mile wide
stands sentinel. This island has two small hills; on
the lesser of these are the ruins of an old fort. The
bay is Gros Ilet Bay which sheltered the British fleet
before the Battle of the Saints, and it was from the walls
of the old fort—known ever since as Fort Rodney—that
the admiral watched with his glass the movements of
the French vessels off Martinique; and it was here that
he was kept informed by a chain of swift schooners of
the offensive preparations which were being hurriedly

PIGEON ISLAND, GROS ILET BAY, ST. LUCIA

pressed forward in Fort Royal Bay some twenty-five miles away.

De Grasse in his flagship, the *Ville de Paris*, was awaiting reinforcements which were daily expected to arrive from France. This *Ville de Paris* was what was then considered a very magnificent vessel. Equipped with one hundred and ten guns, she had been presented by the City of Paris to Louis XV. when the French navy had been reduced to a state of decay at the close of the last war. No pains or expense had been spared to render this noble ship worthy of the great city and of the monarch to whom she was presented. She is indeed said to have cost no less than £176,000 to build and fit out for sea, an immense sum of money to spend on a ship in those days. On board she carried no fewer than 1300 men, while the French fleet as a whole bore an entire train of artillery, with battering cannon and travelling carriages, intended for the attack on Jamaica.

De Grasse's intention had been to sail for San Domingo and to join forces there with the Spaniards, and Rodney, with the object of intercepting the convoy which the French admiral was awaiting, cruised to windward of the French islands from the latitude of Deseada or La Désirade (a small island six miles to the east of Guadeloupe) to that of St. Vincent, keeping a line of frigates still farther to windward. He was, however, outmanœuvred, the French making La Désirade from the north, and by hugging Guadeloupe and Dominica reaching their destination at Martinique on March 20 and 21, 1782.

Rodney now made it his aim to prevent the French

joining hands with their Spanish allies, while de Grasse did all he could to avoid a battle.

So matters stood until April 8. At daybreak on that day the *Alert* brought the news to Gros Ilet that the French fleet, in great force and accompanied by many transports, had been observed leaving Fort Royal Bay with a large convoy, their evident intention being to make a desperate effort to form a junction with the Spanish fleet. This information was at once communicated to the Commander-in-Chief by Sir Charles Douglas, his flag captain, who told him that "God had given him the enemy on the lee bow."

Rodney immediately gave orders to weigh anchor, and by noon the whole of his fleet was clear of Gros Ilet Bay and hotly pursuing the French, who were sighted from the masthead standing away to the northward. Throughout the day the chase was continued, and at nightfall the enemy were seen under the lee of Dominica spreading as much canvas as they could carry in their efforts to elude their pursuers. The English kept steadily on their course, Sir Samuel Hood in the *Barfleur* leading the van, while Sir George Rodney in the *Formidable* commanded the centre division and Sir Francis Drake—a kinsman of the great Elizabethan seafarer—in the *Princessa* brought up the rear division.

At 2 A.M. on the 9th the *St. Albans* hailed the flagship, and reported that the enemy had been sighted by the *Valiant* off the north end of Dominica. The signal for battle was at once hoisted, and the fleet formed in line ahead at two cable lengths apart. Sir

Samuel Hood, assisted by a fair breeze, rapidly closed on the enemy, who fired at his foremost ship the *Alfred*. A partial engagement ensued, which lasted about an hour, during which eight sail of the British van were engaged by fifteen of the enemy, and Captain Bayne of the *Alfred*, a brave officer, was killed. The situation was then relieved by the arrival of Rodney with the centre division.

The French kept well away to windward at what Sir Charles Douglas described as "their much loved cannonading distance," and, helped by a breeze, were able to make off while the English lay becalmed.

During the next two days Rodney continued to shadow his antagonist without, however, being able to bring him to battle. On the morning of the 11th one of de Grasse's vessels was sighted, bearing away for Basseterre, Guadeloupe, where yet another was espied. They were chased, but managed to get in unharmed. Shortly afterwards two more French ships were discerned far away to windward, bearing evident signs of damage from the engagement of the 9th. One was rigging her foreyard and the other a maintop-mast. The signal was given for a general chase, and by the afternoon the *Agamemnon* got so near the two ships that they signalled for assistance and brought down de Grasse *en corps*. The opportunity for which the English had been waiting seemed at last to have arrived. Calling his fleet into close order, Rodney completed his preparations for an immediate action. Till 2 A.M. he stood to southward and then tacked towards the north.

Shortly after sunrise on April 12 the enemy's fleet was sighted to leeward, and it was seen that one of the French ships, with a broken bowsprit and her foremast lying across the forecastle, was being towed by a frigate towards Guadeloupe. She proved to be the hapless *Zélé*, which had been in collision overnight with the flagship and the *Astrée*. The *Valiant* and *Monarch* were hastily sent in chase, whereupon the *Astrée* hoisted signals of distress, which attracted de Grasse and his entire fleet.

Rodney realised that the moment for which he had been waiting had arrived, and recalling the chasing ships he made signal for line of battle on the starboard tack, Admiral Drake leading the van. De Grasse then formed his line of battle on the larboard tack, and the two fleets now slowly approached each other.

Just before eight o'clock in the morning the battle was opened, the *Marlborough*, the leading ship of Drake's division, opening fire on the centre and rear of the French.

The signal for close action at once fluttered from the British flagship, and the fight began in earnest. A heavy fire was kept up on both sides, the British ships sliding down slowly and closely along the enemy's line and under their lee, and pouring in broadside after broadside, which was returned with vigour by the French ships.

At eleven o'clock the sea breeze freshened, and Rodney and Sir Samuel Hood closed up with the enemy's van. The fleets were now sailing parallel and in opposite directions to each other. Rodney in the

Formidable received the fire of eight or nine of de Grasse's ships in succession, but he did not return it until he got well down the line. Then it was that the brilliant manœuvre was performed which gained the day for the British. Lying as close to the wind as he could, Rodney gave instructions for his ship to be steered for a gap in the French line two or three ships astern of the *Ville de Paris*. Sir Charles Douglas at once carried out the order—indeed, many say that it was he who suggested it in the first instance—with precision " angling in upon the enemy, in order to penetrate his line of battle." The *Formidable* then passed right through the enemy's line followed by six ships of the centre division. De Grasse's van was thus separated from his centre, and Rodney by veering his ships brought the French between two fires. The immediate effect of this manœuvre was to throw the French fleet into utter confusion and disorder from end to end. The *Duke*, the *Namur* and the *Formidable* poured their broadsides into four of the French vessels, which were so huddled together that they made " one large single object to fire at."

Barbadians are always popularly supposed to be ubiquitous, and of course one of them was with the British fleet. He was the Hon. Nathan Lucas, a member of the Legislature of Barbados, who was Rodney's guest in the flagship on this memorable day. Lucas was Charles Kingsley's grandfather, and the pity is that he had not his grandson's wonderful gift of writing and did not hand down to us an account of his experience 'tween decks in the

Formidable during the fight. Another man of note who was with the fleet on this eventful day was a young officer, Robert Scott, the eldest brother of Sir Walter Scott, who on the night before the battle composed the following elegy :

> *No more the geese shall cackle on the poop,*
> *No more the bag-pipe through the orlop sound,*
> *No more the Midshipmen, a jovial group,*
> *Shall toast the girls and pass the bottle round.*
> *In death's dark road, at anchor fast they stay,*
> *'Till Heaven's loud signal shall in thunder roar ;*
> *Then starting up, all hands shall quick obey,*
> *Sheet home the topsail, and with speed unmoor.* *

When the battle was at its height the clouds of smoke were so dense that the order to cease firing had perforce to be given, so difficult did it become to discriminate between friend and foe ; but this was only for a few minutes, and as soon as the smoke had cleared away the cannon thundered forth again with redoubled energy.

As the *Formidable* was passing the *Glorieux*, raking her with her broadsides at close range, Douglas is said to have exclaimed, " Behold, Sir George, the Greeks and Trojans contending for the body of Patroclus," a remark to which Rodney characteristically replied, " Damn the Greeks and damn the Trojans ; I have other things to think of." Some little time later, however, he smilingly said to Douglas, " Now, my dear friend, I am at the service of the Greeks and Trojans

* " One Hundred Years Ago," by N. Darnell Davis, 1882.

90

THE BATTLE OF THE SAINTS ON THE GLORIOUS 12TH OF APRIL, 1782

From an engraving by James Fittler after the painting by Richard Paton

and the whole of Homer's ' Iliad,' for the enemy is in confusion and our victory is secure."

The victory of the British was indeed assured. The French made desperate efforts to re-form their broken lines, but all to no purpose. For two hours *Ville de Paris* was hotly engaged by the *Canada*, but the gallant de Grasse resolutely declined to strike his colours, and it was not until Sir Samuel Hood came up in the *Barfleur* and delivered several furious broadsides —the first of which killed no fewer than sixty men— that he was at last compelled to do so. Throughout the fight de Grasse had remained on the quarter-deck, and when *Ville de Paris* was taken, only three men of her fighting strength remained unwounded, of whom he was one.

The rest of the enemy made off to leeward closely pursued by Commodore Affleck in the *Bedford* and other British ships.

When darkness closed in on the glorious April 12 Rodney hove to for the night. Next morning a pursuit was attempted, but the British fleet was becalmed off Guadeloupe, and so the crippled remains of the French fleet managed to reach Cape François under MM. de Bougainville—whose name is perpetuated by the gorgeous flowering creeper, the bougainvillea, so familiar throughout the West Indies—and de Vaudreuil, while four sail of the line reached Curaçao.

The English losses on this memorable day consisted of 253 killed—including Captain Blair of the *Anson* and Lord Robert Manners of the *Resolution*, who succumbed to lockjaw after having had his leg shot off—and 1050 wounded, while it was computed that the French lost 3000 men who were killed and wounded, 400 being killed in the *Ville de Paris* alone.

In all, five French vessels were captured: the *Ville de Paris*, 110 guns, by Sir Samuel Hood in the *Barfleur*; the *Glorieux*, 74; the *César*, which was taken by Captain Inglefield in the *Centaur*; the *Hector*, which fell to Captain Cornwallis of the *Centaur*, a kinsman of the second Lord Cornwallis, who thus retrieved the defeat of his ancestor at Yorktown; and the *Ardent*, while the *Diadème* was sunk. Unfortunately, however, the *César* was lost. A lieutenant and fifty men had been sent to take charge of the vessel, but the four hundred prisoners in her proved more than they could manage. Maddened by drink, these men in their drunken orgies set fire to the ship which blew up, killing the Englishmen aboard her at the time.

Meanwhile the people of Jamaica had for weeks been living in constant fear of attack. The militia had been called out and trade was at a standstill, the inhabitants being over-burdened by heavy taxation imposed to meet the cost of strengthening the defences of the island. Preparations for resisting the threatened invasion were hurried forward, and gangs of slaves were actively occupied, day after day, hewing down trees and blockading the main roads of the island with the trunks.

The anxiety, which was shared by all classes of the community, was increased when, at a meeting of the House of Assembly on April 24, the Governor read a despatch from General Mathews, the Commandant of the troops at St. Lucia, announcing that the opposing fleets had sailed from Martinique and St. Lucia respectively. On the following day, however, the tension was relieved by the arrival of a despatch from Rodney himself announcing his great and crowning victory.

This intelligence was hailed with the greatest manifestations of joy. The black folk are proverbially demonstrative and are certainly not prone to conceal their emotions. It may, therefore, safely be assumed that the scene in Kingston when the good news was communicated to the Assembly was one of unbounded enthusiasm, the church bells ringing, flags flying and the populace shouting itself hoarse in its excitement. All fears of a descent upon the island by the dreaded French and Spanish fleets were removed, and to make the happiness of the people complete there was the prospect of their hero Rodney visiting them. " I am hastening with my whole fleet to the succour of Jamaica," he wrote, "and you may hourly expect me with such ships of my fleet as are in a condition to keep the sea off the east end of your island. Not a few will be obliged to repair to Port Royal."

It may well be imagined that, after the receipt of this gratifying announcement, a close watch was kept for the arrival of the victorious British fleet. The people ' ' not long to wait. On April 29 Rodney's vessels w. e discerned approaching the island. As they came nearer it was seen that they were accompanied by no fewer than nine prizes on which the red cross of St. George now proudly floated over the lilies of France.

Victors and vanquished alike bore evident traces

of the severity of the recent engagement. Their sails were rent, their rigging tangled and their sides shattered by shot. Slowly they made their way past the batteries of Port Royal which, no doubt, thundered forth a salute, and dropped anchor in Kingston Harbour. In the flagship was de Grasse himself, a prisoner.

The people rushed down to the water front to welcome the gallant British sailors, but their joy was tinged with disappointment when they learned that Rodney himself was too ill to come ashore. He had for some time been in indifferent health, and several days elapsed before he had sufficiently recovered to land and to receive the congratulations of the populace, which were embodied in many Addresses.

Meanwhile the shattered vessels of both fleets lay off Port Royal. Never before had the dockyard there been so busy. The French prizes, riddled with shot, had to be patched up preparatory to their voyage to England, and the work was busily hurried forward, as it was appreciated how desirous the people of England would be to see tangible results of the great victory.

Rodney remained at Jamaica until July 22, when he was relieved by Admiral Hugh Pigot, and sailed for England in the *Jupiter*. During his absence Lord North's ministry had left office and had been succeeded by that of Lord Rockingham, whose naval advisers, through jealousy or other motives, disliked Rodney; and, taking advantage of the clamour raised by the merchants over the seizure of their stores and merchandise at St. Eustatius in 1781, the new ministry

94

decided to recall the hero and actually sent Admiral Pigot to supersede him. News of the crowning victory reached London the very day after Pigot's departure, but it was too late to intercept him.

In a letter to Mr. Stephens of the Admiralty, Rodney wrote from aboard the *Formidable* at sea on April 14, 1782:

" Sir

" It has pleased God, out of his divine providence, to grant to his Majesty's arms a most complete victory over the fleet of his enemy, commanded by the Count de Grasse, who is himself captured, with the *Ville de Paris* and four other ships of the fleet, besides one sunk in the action. This important victory was obtained the 12th instant, after a battle which lasted, with unremitting fury, from seven in the morning till half-past six in the evening, when the setting sun put an end to the contest.

" That the British flag may for every flourish in every quarter of the globe is the most ardent wish of him who has the honour of being, with great regard,

" Sir,

" Your most obedient, humble Servant,

" G. B. RODNEY."

Popular feeling at once veered round in favour of Rodney, and when he arrived in England he was received with great rejoicings and every mark of favour. The victory had restored the prestige of England, and the King showed his appreciation by raising the victorious admiral to the peerage as Baron Rodney, of Stoke Rodney, while Parliament voted £2000 a year to him

95

and to his successors for his gallant conduct during the war. Hood was given an Irish peerage, and Admiral Drake and Commodore Affleck were rewarded for their share in the victory with baronetcies.

It may well be imagined that the arrival of the French prizes from the West Indies was eagerly awaited. Alas, however, only one of them was destined to reach its destination. On the homeward voyage they encountered a terrible hurricane off the Banks of Newfoundland on September 17, and every single ship, with the exception of the *Ardent*, foundered.

The homeward bound fleet consisting of nine ships of the line, the *Pallas*, a frigate of 36 guns, and about 100 sail of merchantmen, sailed from Bluefields at the western end of Jamaica, where they had gathered under the command of Admiral Graves in the *Ramillies*, a seventy-four. Before they actually left the island the number of ships of the line was reduced to seven, the *Ardent*—fortunately for those on board her, as subsequent events proved,—having sprung a leak which necessitated her remaining behind, while the *Jason* for some cause or other was also detained.

As part of the convoy was bound for New York, the admiral shaped his course in a more northerly direction than he would otherwise have done, with the result that the fleet soon experienced bad weather. On September 8 they ran into a heavy gale in which the *Caton*, a sixty-four, sprang a leak and hoisting signals of distress was sent under the charge of the *Pallas* to Halifax. Before the bad weather came on the *Hector*, under the command of Captain Bourchier, had fallen so

THE CHAPEL BELL   A SENTRY'S CLOCK

TWO RELICS FROM THE VILLE DE PARIS

(*See page* 100)

far astern that she lost company with the rest of the
fleet and never regained it.

During the afternoon of September 16, while the
fleet and convoy were off the Banks of Newfoundland, they encountered a terrific gale from the E.S.E.,
which blew with increasing violence throughout the
evening and night. At three on the following morning
the wind shifted suddenly, and a sharp squall came on
from the N.N.W., accompanied by a torrential down-
pour of rain, which was characterised by the oldest
seaman in the fleet as the very worst which he had ever
experienced.

By ten o'clock in the morning the *Ramillies* was in a
pitiful plight. She was leaking badly, and as she had
six feet of water in her hold it was judged best to abandon
her. Her crew were accordingly transhipped to one of
the merchantmen and she was set on fire, Captain
Moriarty leaving her a few minutes only before she blew
up. The fury of the gale may be judged from the fact
that the *Centaur*, though under bare poles when the
squall came on, was immediately laid upon her beam-
ends, while the water burst through her hold and
between decks. It was not until her masts had been
swept overboard and her rudder carried away that the
vessel was righted, and then she regained her equili-
brium with such suddenness that her guns broke loose,
causing further damage and confusion.

The water raced along the decks carrying everything
away, and the officers who had rushed up the com-
panion ways in the scantiest of attire were left with no
clothes to wear when dawn broke on a scene of wreckage

and distress. By dint of great exertions the vessel was
kept afloat until September 23, but on that day, it
appearing that all efforts to save her must prove fruit-
less and that she was filling fast and gradually sinking,
she was abandoned, though not before the water had
burst through on to the orlop deck.

The sailors lashed themselves to gratings and rafts
which were hurriedly prepared, but only a few of them
were saved. Captain Inglefield, and the master and ten
men shoved off from the wreck in a pinnace. They had
no compass or quadrant, no sail and only a scanty supply
of provisions—a bag of bread, a small ham, 2 lbs. of
pork, some French cordials, and about two quarts of
water being all that was available. For days the
sufferings of these unfortunate men were intense. They
encountered fierce gales and heavy seas, but never for a
moment did their courage desert them. While some
baled out the boat, others sat at the bottom of it, and
obtained what little rest they could waist deep in water.
A blanket attached to a stretcher served as a very inadequate sail; and to keep their spirits up Captain Inglefield
insisted upon every man in turn either telling a story or
singing a song. Luckily the weather moderated, but on
the fifth morning the bread was damaged by salt water,
and it became necessary to put every man upon a rigid
allowance of food. A ship's biscuit was broken into
twelve pieces every twelve hours, and distributed without respect to rank; and twice a day a portion of water
was served out to each man after being carefully
measured in the neck of a bottle in which the cork had
been left—the only receptacle available.

THE BATTLE OF THE SAINTS

On the fifteenth day the quartermaster died and the men were reduced to their last day's supply of bread, while only a single bottle of water was left.

The strength of the survivers was now reduced to such a low ebb that Captain Inglefield could no longer induce the sailors to sing. The outlook seemed hopeless indeed. God was, however, merciful, and, on the day which followed, shortly after the very last biscuit had been broken up and distributed, land was sighted. It proved to be the island of Fayal, one of the Azores, and that same night the exhausted survivors from the wreck of the *Centaur* set foot on shore—which they never expected to do again.

Of many vessels of Admiral Graves' fleet no more was heard. Few survived the appalling gales of that September. The *Ville de Paris* and the *Glorieux* were both steered in the direction of the Azores, but neither vessel succeeded in reaching those islands.

Some weeks later a Danish merchantman, returning from the West Indies, picked up a man named Wilson who was floating on a piece of wreckage, and he declared that he had seen the *Glorieux* go down. It is certain that a similar fate must also have befallen the *Ville de Paris*. She was never heard of again.

Two sons of Flora Macdonald were on board the flagship when she foundered, and with the exception of the seaman Wilson not one of the officers or crew was saved.

Great was the grief in England when the news of the disaster which had overtaken the homeward-bound fleet became known, and keen was the disappointment of the people at not having the opportunity of seeing the much-talked of *Ville de Paris* after all. An old bell which used to hang outside the chapel on board, a highly ornate clock, the hands of which were adjusted from time to time by a sentry, two bronze cannon—to which reference is made below—and a few other trophies of a similar kind were all that remained of the equipment of this superb ship.

The people of Jamaica were not slow to mark their sense of appreciation of the service which Rodney had rendered their island.

The House of Assembly unanimously resolved to write to Stephen Fuller, Esq., the agent of the island in England, asking him " to apply to the most eminent artist in England, to prepare an elegant marble statue of Lord Rodney with a handsome pedestal to the same, to be erected in Spanish Town in commemoration of the glorious victory obtained by that gallant commander and the brave officers serving under him over the French Fleet, on the 12th day of April, 1782." Premiums for designs to be approved by the Royal Academy were to be offered, and the most eminent statuary employed to carry them out.*

The Council of the Academy, however, instead of inviting public competition, requested Bacon, Carlini, Nollekens, Tyler and Wilton to prepare designs, but of these only Bacon and Tyler submitted models. The design by Bacon being adjudged the best, that sculptor was commissioned to execute the statue. It

---

* " Sculpture in Jamaica," by Frank Cundall, F.S.A.

THE RODNEY MEMORIAL, SPANISH TOWN, JAMAICA

As it appeared on Emancipation Day, August 1, 1838. From a lithograph by R. Cartwright

took over six years to complete, and its arrival in 1790 was followed by a remarkable squabble over the possession of this work of art.

The people of Kingston and Port Royal, hearing a report that the statue was to be erected at Spanish Town, laid a petition before the House of Assembly asking that it might be placed on the Parade at Kingston. The petition runs: "Conscious that such an ornament can only be adapted to decorate a place equally conspicuous in point of situation, and convenient with respect to proximity to those harbours which his victory graced, they have anticipated the public approbation of seeing his statue erected in the centre of the first commercial town in the West Indies, and solicit us to improve every advantage of position, as well as to add every possible embellishment, to this testimony of public gratitude. They some time ago subscribed a large sum of money for the purpose of conveying water from Hope River to the Parade, Kingston, by means of which they propose to form a spacious basin to surround the statue; and have lately subscribed a further considerable sum to assist in erecting it, but are penetrated with the greatest concern to find a report which prevails, of its being intended to be placed in Spanish Town."

On the consideration of this petition the House, which then met at Spanish Town, was equally divided, and the statue was only lost to Kingston by the casting-vote of the acting Speaker. A sum of £3000 was then voted for the erection of a suitable building to shelter the statue. This suitable building now stands

101

on the north side of the stately square in the centre of
Spanish Town, on the west of which is the old King's
House, the former official residence of the Governors of
Jamaica. An ornate plaster temple with a cupola and
lanthorn supported by open arches and connected with
the neighbouring buildings by a colonnade shelters
Bacon's masterpiece.

Rodney is represented as clad in a short-sleeved
tunic. Over his right arm he has a cloak, on his feet
are sandals, and from his neck is suspended a Medusa's
head. The pedestal is inscribed :—

GEORG. BRYDG. RODNEY

BARON RODNEY

NAVAL. PRAEL. VICTORI

PRID. ID. APRILIS

A.D. MDCCLXXXII

BRITANN. PACEM REST.

D.D.D. S.P.Q. JAMAICENSIS

This may roughly be rendered :—

TO GEORGE BRYDGES RODNEY

BARON RODNEY

VICTOR IN A SEA FIGHT

ON THE DAY BEFORE THE IDES OF APRIL

IN THE YEAR OF OUR LORD 1782.

HE RESTORED PEACE TO BRITAIN.

THE LEGISLATURE AND THE PEOPLE OF JAMAICA

PRESENTED [THIS MEMORIAL]

On either side of the statue is a bronze cannon of

102

exquisite workmanship. One bears the name "Le Précipice" and the other "Le Modeste," and it is recorded that they were cast at Donai, in 1748, by Jean Maritz. These handsome cannon formed part of the armament of the *Ville de Paris,* to the magnificence of whose equipment they bear striking testimony. They bear the inscription :—

ULTIMA RATIO REGUM

PLURIBUS NEC IMPAR

LOUIS CHARLES DE BOURBON

COMTE D'EU

DUC D'AUMALE

De Grasse was the first Commander-in-Chief to be sent prisoner to England since Marshal Tallard was brought to London after the Battle of Blenheim. Rodney's victory enabled Great Britain to secure a termination of the war. As far as the West Indies are concerned, the result of the victory was to retain Jamaica and other islands under the Flag, and to regain the islands that had been captured by the French during the war. It seems strange that so fateful an event should not be commemorated year by year by the colonies that profited by it. As in the case of the Battle of Trafalgar, there might be an annual commemoration of the notable victory in a spirit of thankfulness for preservation from dire calamity, rather than in one of triumph over a gallant foe, who is now a fast friend.

103

CHAPTER V

CHAGUARAMAS BAY, TRINIDAD

IN the ten years which immediately preceded the cession of Trinidad to England, that island, though actually Spanish, was, to all intent and purposes, a French colony. Under the rule of Spain it had never enjoyed any substantial measure of prosperity, and repeated failures of the cocoa crop reduced the inhabitants, who were too apathetic and indolent even to catch the fish with which the waters surrounding the island abound, to a state of poverty bordering on destitution. It is indeed recorded that on one occasion the people, who only numbered a few hundreds, were in such straits that, in a petition to the King, they complained that they could only go to Mass once a year " in clothes borrowed from each other." The members, too, of the Illustrious Board of the Cabildo, a body which exercised administrative besides municipal functions, and comprised " two Alcades, three Regidors, a Procurador-General, an Alcade of the Santa Hermanadad, a Gaoler and a Quadrillion who bore the canopy in church," had, according, at least, to an old newspaper, only one pair of small clothes among them.

104

CHAGUARAMAS BAY, TRINIDAD

It was left to M. Rome de St. Laurent, an enterprising Frenchman from Grenada, to build up the
fortunes of Trinidad. Recognising, during a visit
which he paid to the island in 1780, the remarkable
fertility of its soil, he proceeded at once to Madrid
and sought the permission of the King to colonise it
with his own countrymen. His mission proved successful and three months after the Peace of Paris his
Catholic Majesty signed a Cedula for the encourage-
ment of the peopling of Trinidad. Shortly afterwards the document was translated into French and
English and acted upon.

It was stipulated by Article 1 of the Cedula that
all intending settlers should "sufficiently prove to the
Government" that they were of the Roman Catholic
persuasion; but this did not prevent large numbers
of disreputable people with no religious convictions
whatever availing themselves of Spain's hospitality.
It was easy for them to declare that they were
Roman Catholics, and the new arrivals were not submitted to any very rigorous cross-examination.

A large influx of French from the neighbouring
islands, leavened with Irish and runaway slaves,
ensued and, in the course of a few years, the respectable Spanish inhabitants were outnumbered. French
became the prevailing language in the place and
Trinidad remained Spanish in name only.

In his eagerness to populate the island St. Laurent
showed, unfortunately, little discrimination and Port
of Spain—which, owing to a ridiculous dispute between
the Governor and the Cabildo as to where they

105

should meet, succeeded San Josef de Oruna, now St. Joseph, as capital—became a place of refuge for the most worthless and good-for-nothing characters in the West Indies.

At the outbreak of the French Revolution many Royalists from the neighbouring islands fled to Trinidad seeking protection under the Spanish flag. Victor Hugues, the friend of Robespierre, arrived among the islands to preach and also to put into practice the revolutionary doctrines of the Convention. The guillotine was set up in the market places in the French islands, and the streets were soon running with blood. The cry of Liberty and Equality was raised, slaves were released and nowhere was the revolution more popular or more vigorously carried out than in the West Indies.

In 1795 Hugues had little difficulty in recapturing St. Lucia, which had only been taken from France by Admiral Jervis—afterwards Lord St. Vincent—in the preceding year, when the Duke of Kent, father of Queen Victoria, stormed the Morne Fortuné and planted the English colours on the summit. Grenada was soon in the throes of a rebellion started by Julien Fédon, a coloured planter, who massacred the Governor Ninian Home and many other notable residents; in St. Vincent the Caribs rose under Chatoyer and Duvallée and, with the aid of the French, devastated the island, burning the cane fields and pillaging the houses.

The behaviour of the French residents in Trinidad, with the exception of the Royalists, was at this juncture simply outrageous. They were kept informed by the privateers that infested the Caribbean of the happenings in the other islands which they followed with wild enthusiasm, and, on the slightest provocation, they would hoist the tricolour and parade the streets singing the Marseillaise, Çaira and other revolutionary songs. The Spaniards were powerless to put a stop to these proceedings and it was an open secret that only the arrival in the Gulf of Admiral Don Gabriel de Aristizabal with a Spanish squadron on his way to San Domingo to remove the remains of Christopher Columbus to Spain prevented an actual insurrection.

The Governor of Trinidad, Don Josef Maria Chacon, was quite unable to cope with the situation. Though a man of great talent, indefatigable activity and superior accomplishments, he was lamentably weak and declined to take the drastic measures against the disorderly people which the admiral advocated, and the latter therefore proceeded on his voyage to San Domingo.

While the island was in this unsettled state Sir Ralph Abercromby arrived in the West Indies with a force of 15,000 men with the object of retaking St. Lucia and of pacifying Grenada and St. Vincent.

Finding that his operations were seriously hampered by some French privateers which were conveying munitions of war and provisions to the rebels, besides harassing our merchantmen, he despatched the *Alarm*, a frigate of 32 guns commanded by Captain Vaughan, and the *Zebra*, sloop of war, of which Captain Skinner was in command, in pursuit. Driven from their hiding places among that maze of islands known as the Grenadines, the privateers, assured of the sympathy of many of the inhabitants of Trinidad, sought refuge in the Gulf of Paria, believing that in that almost land-locked sea they would be safe from their pursuers.

Captain Vaughan was, however, determined to attack them, and he accordingly sent Captain Skinner through the Bocas to Port of Spain to obtain the Governor's permission to attack the privateers in Spanish waters.

These Bocas, it should be explained, are the narrow " mouths," or straits, which give access from the open sea to the almost land-locked Gulf of Paria. Trinidad, which lies off the coast of Venezuela, has sometimes been compared with a hide stretched out, or—more appropriately, perhaps—with a turtle. At the four corners it has promontories, of which those at the north-west and south-west are extended towards the mainland almost enclosing a magnificent sheet of water —the Gulf of Paria—on which, one would imagine, all the navies of the world might safely ride at anchor at the same time. The northerly promontory breaks off into a series of rugged islands, Monos or Monkey Island, Huevos or Egg Island, and Chacachacare, whose peculiar name is of Indian origin. These islands form the four northern Bocas or straits which are called respectively Monos, Huevos, Navios and the Boca Grande. At the south of the island there is only one Boca, the Boca Sierpe or Serpent's Mouth, through

108

which Columbus entered the Gulf after sighting the three peaks in Moruga, now known as the Three Sisters, and discovering Trinidad.

Through the northern straits the current races like a mill stream, and before the days of steam it was no easy matter to negotiate the mouths unless the wind was favourable. Ships would sometimes spend hours beating about and battling against the current in their efforts to gain the placid waters of the gulf beyond. Nowadays the Bocas present no feature of difficulty to the experienced navigator, and the traveller finds the passage through them all too short. As he enters the Gulf the scenery is grand, almost beyond description. Behind him rise the beetling crags and precipices of the mysterious islands of the Bocas. To his left is a range of mountains densely clothed with tropical forest from the water's edge to the very summit. As the steamer proceeds along the coast the scene gains in breadth and majesty. Two more islands are passed, those of Gasparillo and Gaspar Grande, the latter of which, once strongly fortified, closes in Chaguaramas Bay, and the steamer then glides by a fairy-like archipelago known to countless pleasure seekers from Port of Spain as the Five Islands, and formerly called Los Cotorros or the Parrots, the peer of which not even the Italian lakes can boast.

About two hours later Port of Spain, admirably situated at the angle of the north-west promontory already mentioned, is reached.

Skinner arrived at night and dropping anchor off Port of Spain landed, and was at once conducted to

109

Government House, where he was granted an interview by the Governor in the presence of his secretary, Don Diego Meany.

Chacon, after reading Captain Vaughan's despatches, admitted that the forces at his disposal were altogether insufficient to protect the shipping in the Gulf. He added, however, that though he was anxious that the privateers, which were manned by runaway slaves and revolutionaries from Martinique, Dominica, St. Vincent and Grenada, might be destroyed, the English must respect the laws of neutrality. As to what followed, some doubt exists. According to Mr. E. L. Joseph, who relates the episode in his " History of Trinidad," Chacon told Captain Skinner that the *Mary*, an English merchantman, which had been for some days loaded and ready to sail, had been prevented from doing so through fear of capture. Next morning the *Zebra* weighed anchor and started to sail out of the Bocas to rejoin the *Alarm*. The privateers, seven or eight in number, mistaking her for the *Mary*, gave chase. Skinner, pretending that he was endeavouring to escape, drew them on until they were in an advantageous position, and then, just as the men from one of them were endeavouring to board the *Zebra*, he suddenly tacked and fired a broadside on them, a manœuvre which proved so successful that in about three-quarters of an hour every one of the vessels was either sunk, burnt or driven ashore. Most of their crews succeeded in reaching Port of Spain where, in a great state of indignation at having been attacked in neutral waters, they joined the French Republicans, who were now

110

practically masters of Trinidad, and swore vengeance against the English. Such is Mr. Joseph's story of the affair.

M. Pierre Gustave Louis Borde, on the other hand, discredits the story about the *Mary*,* which he declares must have been invented to give an appearance of honesty to an unjustifiable act of war ; but without questioning which authority is correct, it will suffice here to record that on one point they are in agreement, and that is with regard to the destruction of the privateers, which was complete.

The *Zebra* now sailed to leeward, and on receiving Skinner's report Captain Vaughan, in the *Alarm*, entered the Bocas, anchored off Port of Spain and after paying his respects to Chacon visited the leading Spanish and English settlers, by whom he was well received.

One evening during his stay in the town some of his officers were visiting a Welsh lady named Griffith at a house in the thoroughfare now called Frederick Street, the busy shopping centre of Trinidad, when the crew of the boats which were waiting at the wharf to take them aboard again were insulted by some of the vanquished sailors from the privateers, who, as already stated, had found their way back to the town. A quarrel ensued and angry words soon led to blows, the bluejackets making good use of their oars and boat-hooks. Hearing the noise the officers drew their swords and rushed to

* " Histoire de l'Ile de la Trinidad sous le Gouvernement Espagnol," par M. Pierre Gustave Louis Borde. Paris, Maison neuve, 1882. Vol. ii., 225.

the assistance of their men. A general mêlée ensued, the French Republicans eagerly joining in the fray with cries of " Vive la Republique," "A bas les Anglais," etc. Being completely surrounded, and finding themselves cut off from their boats, the sailors of the *Alarm* charged through the crowd and took refuge in a house at the corner of Marine Square, which was then called the Campus Martius. Up to this point no blood had been shed, but shots were now exchanged and the ship's surgeon was seriously wounded. The whole town was soon in an uproar. Don Juan Jurado de Lianes, with the few Spanish troops which he was able to collect, did his best to break up the mob without bloodshed, but it was with the greatest difficulty that he could restrain his men from firing on the French revolutionaries, whose arrogant and insulting attitude rendered them particularly unpopular. Haranguing the mob from a window of the house, he managed to gain sufficient time to enable the British sailors to escape over a wall at the back and regain their boats. Shouting " Mort aux Anglais ! Ouvrez les portes ! Ouvrez les portes ou nous les enforcerons," the rabble surrounded the house, and an entrance was soon effected. It was now dark, but lanterns having been sent for and obtained, a search was made for the English. Only the surgeon was found, however, and though the French cursed him freely he was not otherwise molested. Disappointed in their quest, the enraged mob then returned to the main streets singing the Marseillaise and their other revolutionary songs.

Captain Vaughan, nearly mad with anger, decided

to wreak speedy vengeance on the French, and next morning at daybreak every available boat left the frigate with as many seamen and marines as it could carry, armed to the teeth with boarding pikes, pistols and swords. The men were formed up on the beach, and the order to advance having been given, colours were unfurled and the sailors proceeded towards the town. They had not gone far, however, before they were stopped by a Spanish officer, who asked Vaughan what he meant by thus violating the laws of neutrality. Vaughan replied that it was his intention to chastise the French. The Spaniard, realising the helplessness of his position, then offered Vaughan his sword, but that officer refused to take it, saying that he would not accept the arms of a brave man who was doing his duty.

With the drums and fifes gaily playing " Britons Strike Home," the expedition now proceeded on its way until, a little farther on, it was again stopped, this time by a deputation of the English inhabitants and French Royalists, who warmly urged Vaughan to return, pointing out that any breach of the peace would recoil disastrously on the respectable residents of Port of Spain. Their entreaties were without effect, and the men of the *Alarm* continued their march up the town.

Meanwhile the French Republicans had assembled in considerable force, and arming their slaves and negroes prepared to meet the Englishmen. Chacon was in a desperate plight. He had a mere handful of men under his command, but by a quick march

113

he managed to intercept the opposing parties, which were now within gunshot of each other. Speaking in English, he asked Vaughan what he meant by this outrage to the flag of a friendly power. Vaughan replied that he had no intention of insulting or injuring the hospitable Spaniards, but that he was determined to avenge the insult offered to his colleagues by the French. Chacon then said he would not permit the dominion of his Sovereign to be thus violated. The English should advance no farther without forcing a passage through his men, and if they did that the whole of the French would be upon them, and both the Spanish and the English would be massacred in the streets.

A hurried consultation among the English officers then ensued, and after a brief conference Vaughan saluted Chacon, faced his men about and marched them down to their boats, the Republicans following and hooting, while the drums and fifes played the " Rogue's March." On the same day there was violent rioting in Port of Spain, and the English and Irish had to flee to the country, where they were compelled to remain for some weeks.

Thus ended an episode which formed one of the principal causes for the declaration of war made by Spain against England five months later, on October 5, 1796. The other principal reasons were Admiral Hood's conduct at Toulon, and his attacking Corsica without first intimating his intention of doing so to the Spanish officer who was with him at Toulon. After reciting these and other matters for complaint,

GASPAR GRANDE AND LITTLE GASPAREE

CHAGUARAMAS BAY, TRINIDAD

the Declaration went on to say: "Moreover, Captain General Vaughan, commodore of the *Alarm*, behaved in a manner equally insolent and scandalous in the island of Trinidad, where he landed with drums beating and flags flying to attack the French and to avenge the injuries he pretended to have received."

After reducing St. Lucia, of which he appointed General Moore—afterwards Sir John Moore, the hero of Corunna—Governor, subduing Grenada and St. Vincent, and capturing the Dutch colonies of Demerara, Essequibo and Berbice, which now form British Guiana, Abercromby returned to England for the summer of 1796; but in the autumn he again went out to the West Indies, and immediately after the declaration of war by Spain he received instructions to attack Trinidad, if he could do so without exposing the British islands to danger.

These instructions ran: "The Island of Trinidad is pointed out as the source of great mischief to the British Islands, being a shelter for privateers who annoy their trade, and as affording an asylum for bad people of every description, who man the privateers and row boats which make depredations upon the coast, carrying off slaves and property; it is therefore recommended to Sir Ralph Abercromby, if he can collect a sufficient force without exposing the British Islands, to make an attack upon Trinidad, and if the force he can spare should not be sufficient to keep possession after he has taken it, to make the attack notwithstanding, for the purpose of destroying or carrying away all military stores and arms that he may find there, and to seize upon and send to England the brigands and mischievous people who made that Island their home."

Trinidad was not now so defenceless as it had been when Vaughan visited it in the preceding year. Towards the end of 1796, a Spanish squadron, consisting of the *San Vincente*, 84 guns, the *Villardo*, 74, the *Arrogant*, 74, the *San Damaso*, 74, and the frigate *Santa Cecilia*, under the command of Admiral Don Sebastian Ruiz de Apodaca, reached the Gulf from Cadiz on its way to Cartagena with 700 military recruits for that town.

A descent by the English upon the island being now momentarily expected, Apodaca, yielding to the solicitations of Governor Chacon, permitted these raw and undisciplined men to be landed to defend Port of Spain, and then brought his fleet to anchor in Chaguaramas Bay under the shelter of two forts which had been erected on the island of Gaspar Grande. There their troubles began. A violent epidemic of yellow fever broke out among the sailors in the overcrowded and ill-ventilated vessels, with fatal results. So grave was the outbreak that as many as thirty men died in a single day, their bodies being consigned to the deep off Gaspar Grande. Face to face with this terrifying visitation, and debilitated by sickness, the crews became quite demoralised, and Admiral Apodaca was anxious to sail for Puerto Cabello on the Main to escape attack from the British. Chacon, however, persuaded him to stay, pointing out that if he did not do so there would be no possible means of defending the island.

Apodaca accordingly caused an old fort on Gaspar Grande, mounting 20 guns and three mortars, to be repaired, and remained at anchor under its walls.

On February 12, 1797, Admiral Henry Harvey sailed from Martinique in his flagship, the *Prince of Wales*, with Abercromby and his staff on board, for Carriacou, one of the Grenadines, the rendezvous of the fleet. He arrived there on the following morning, and two days later (on the 15th) the fleet, which comprised the flagship, four 74's—the *Bellona*, *Vengeance*, *Invincible* and *Alfred*—and fifteen other vessels, including the *Surett Castle* (an armed East Indiaman), a transport and a bomb vessel, set sail for Trinidad, having on board a force of upwards of 7000 men, drawn from the Queen's Regiment, the Buffs, the 14th, 38th, 53rd and 60th Regiments, the Royal Artillery and Hompesch's and Lowenstein's Jagers.

On the afternoon of February 16 this imposing fleet entered the Bocas, headed by the flagship, which was piloted by a negro named Sharper. The transports convoyed by the *Arethusa*, the *Thorn* and the *Zebra* sailing well to southward of Gaspar Grande and out ot range of the guns of the fort, beat up to Port of Spain, and anchored near the Five Islands.

The news of the approach of the English reached Port of Spain in the morning, and from an early hour the sea front was crowded with people anxiously watching the Bocas through which the hostile fleet would come, and, in the afternoon, ship after ship was seen flying the dreaded flag of England. The Republicans were dismayed; but the Royalists rejoiced at the

117

prospect of being saved from greater indignities at the hands of the disreputable inhabitants.

Apodaca was on shore when the alarm was sounded, and he hastened to seek advice from the Governor, who urged him to rejoin his ships and to destroy the English transports at all costs. Promising to do so, the admiral regained his flagship at noon, but then his courage failed him and he never left the shelter of Gaspar Grande.

The day being well advanced when they entered the Gulf, Harvey and Abercromby, aware of the numerical superiority of their vessels to those of the enemy, decided not to make the attack until morning, and this decision, as events turned out, deprived them of the opportunity of testing conclusions with the Spaniards. Throughout the night, the *Alarm*, the *Favourite* and the *Victorieuse* patrolled the Bocas to keep any of the enemy from leaving the Gulf, while the remainder of the fleet formed up in a half circle round Chaguaramas Bay in order to prevent the escape of the Spanish fleet.

A few hours before dawn on the morning of February 17 the excited crowds which had waited throughout the night on the beach at Port of Spain saw an ominous glare in the sky beyond the headland of Punta Gorda that hid the rival fleets from their view. It was plain that some disaster had overtaken one of the ships. A series of explosions then occurred, and it seemed evident that a fierce battle was in progress; the people were very soon panic-stricken on learning from Apodaca, who reached the town soon after 9 o'clock, that all the proud Spanish ships except one—the *San Damaso* —had been destroyed without the English firing a shot.

118

THE DESTRUCTION OF THE SPANISH FLEET IN CHAGUARAMAS BAY, TRINIDAD

From a painting by Nathaniel Pocock presented to Admiral Harvey

CHAGUARAMAS BAY, TRINIDAD

Overnight Apodaca, realising the hopelessness of his position, had called his captains together to a council of war, and they decided to destroy their vessels by fire rather than allow them to be captured by the English. In the small hours of the morning, Apodaca himself set the cowardly example, strewing resin and other combustibles on the deck of his flagship.

The ships, which burned with great fury, were abandoned and sank at their moorings, the *San Damaso* alone being saved through the courage of the sailors of the *Bellona* and the *Invincible*, who succeeded in extinguishing the flames and making the vessel a prize.

Having silenced the forts on Gaspar Grande, a proceeding which did not require any great expenditure of powder and shot, Abercromby decided to make an immediate advance upon Port of Spain, and before noon a landing was effected at Murucapo, on what was then a sugar estate belonging to the Devenish family and is now known to every visitor to Trinidad as the East Indian village.

The discipline of the troops was admirable, and the only irregularity of which they were guilty was when they broke into a boiling house, or sugar factory, and distillery on the estate and proceeded to make grog on a large scale, by emptying two hogsheads of sugar and three puncheons of rum into a well, and then drawing up the beverage by means of a bucket.* With the men General Abercromby was deservedly popular, for he was the first general to equip his soldiers with clothes suited

* " History of Trinidad," by E. L. Joseph.

to the tropics. Until his arrival in the West Indies the troops wore the same uniforms they were accustomed to wear on parade at home. Now, however, they were suitably attired, and this enabled them quickly to approach Port of Spain.

They encountered little opposition. On nearing the spot where St. James' Barracks now stand they met Lieutenant Don Juan Tornos, of the Royal Spanish Navy, who, with fifty men, had been sent out to reconnoitre, but that officer quickly retired on finding the English in force. Abercromby then, after passing the gorge of the Maraval Valley, skirted the base of the hills and entered Port of Spain, only to find that Chacon had already left. After trying in vain to rally his meagre forces the unfortunate Governor had sent all the archives and documents of state to San Josef and had retired beyond the Laventille Hills.

Resistance was useless, and the final scene was soon enacted. Abercromby sent a message to Chacon calling upon him to surrender, couched in the following terms: " Say to the Governor that I see with sorrow that his troops are without hope of being able to carry out his wishes; that the undeniable superiority of the force under my command has rendered me master of the town, and that he is surrounded on all sides, both by sea and land, without the slightest chance of assistance. There is no possibility of resistance with such unequal forces, and before causing a considerable amount of bloodshed without any hope of ultimate success, I beg him to name a place of conference. I offer him an honourable capitulation, such as is due to

120

good and faithful soldiers who otherwise will be sacrificed in vain."

After a brief consultation with his officers Chacon agreed to give up the island, and on the following day, February 18, he met Abercromby and Harvey in the drawing-room of the residence of Valsayn Estate— now the Government Stock Farm—and signed the Articles of Capitulation. So after being a Spanish possession for nearly three hundred years Trinidad passed under the flag of England.

The Spanish troops were permitted to march out with the honours of war, and a few days after the capitulation Don Josef Maria Chacon left the island, never to return.

On arriving at Cadiz he and Apodaca were immediately placed under arrest, and in May in the following year (1798) they were tried by a Council of War and, after the examination of a great number of witnesses, both were honourably acquitted. This was not however the end of their troubles. The French Republicans were determined to be avenged against the ex-Governor, who they believed had bargained with the hated English and had played the part of a traitor. They accordingly raised subscriptions for his prosecution, and sent many memorials home urging that he might be punished for not defending the colony.

An emissary was sent to Paris where he invoked the assistance of Buonaparte, who was at this time First Consul, and three years after the acquittal of Chacon an order was issued declaring that as the late Governor did not defend the island of Trinidad as he might have done, and as Apodaca destroyed the ships under his command precipitately, they both should have their commissions taken away, and that Chacon should be banished for ever and Apodaca suspended for a period of four years.

Chacon retired to Portugal, and it was not until he was infirm and nearing the end of his days that his case was reopened by his nephew, an officer in the Spanish navy. Yielding to his request the matter was referred to unprejudiced lawyers, who arrived at the conclusion that Chacon was an injured man and guiltless of the charges on which he had been convicted.

The nephew crossed the frontier to convey to Chacon the news of his recall from banishment, but it was too late. He found the unfortunate man on his death-bed in a wretched Portuguese inn. Chacon never set foot on Spanish soil again.

For many years after the capture of Trinidad the charred and blackened hulls of the Spanish ships could be seen deep down in the waters of Chaguaramas Bay, and the rumour went abroad that they contained much treasure and specie. A party of enterprising Americans hearing of this were determined to try to recover it. Arriving at Port of Spain in a schooner they opened up negotiations with Governor Keate with this object in view, and were given permission to salve the contents of the vessels on condition that a proportion of any profits which they might make were handed over to the Government of Trinidad. These terms were accepted and salvage operations were begun, a native policeman being attached to the party to watch the proceedings on behalf of Trinidad. It is said that no policeman ever had a happier time! He was entertained royally by the visitors—so royally, indeed, that all he could remember afterwards was what he had been given to eat and to drink. What treasure the Americans secured history does not relate, but one thing is certain, and that is that all the Trinidad Government received was a barge-load or two of old copper and two small guns, which for years guarded the gardens of the old Government House. Communication with Gasparee was not then as frequent as it is now, and one day it occurred to the Governor that it would be desirable to ascertain how the treasure hunt was proceeding. A boat was sent down to Chaguaramas Bay to find out, but no trace of the Americans could be found. Without a word they had flitted, and it will probably never be known whether they left laden with treasure or disgusted by an unprofitable search for visionary doubloons and plate.

CHAPTER VI

THE DIAMOND ROCK

About half a mile from the Point du Diamant on the south coast of the French West Indian island of Martinique, a huge mass of basaltic rock rises abruptly from the sea. In appearance it closely resembles Ailsa Craig, the form of which is familiar to all visitors to the West of Scotland. Some writers have described it as being like a haystack; but, owing to its somewhat prismatic shape, it has been known to generations of sailors as the Diamond Rock. To passengers to and from the more northerly of the Leeward Islands the rock is always a source of great interest, for it is connected with one of the most brilliant episodes of our naval history.

There is also a legend attached to the rock. The good people of Martinique seriously believed that it was inhabited by tritons. Moreau de Jonnès, in his delightful Aventures de Guèrre,* tells how in 1671 Governor Baas sent to the Académie des Sciences for publication in their records a statement made by an

* "Aventures de Guèrre au temps de la République et du Consulat," par A. Moreau de Jonnès, Paris, 1893, p. 434.

inhabitant describing a triton, which made the Diamond its home. The existence of this monster, half man and half fish, was vouched for by a procès verbal, signed by trustworthy witnesses, and de Jonnès naïvely adds: "A picture of him engraved in copperplate leaves no room for doubting that under the régime of the great King Louis XIV. there were on the coasts of Martinique, as in mythological times, Tritons and undoubtedly also Sirens." But the cosmographers in those days generally embellished their work with such creatures, the appearance of which upon maps and charts is no longer accepted as proof of their existence.

Alas, however, de Jonnès tells this legend to belittle the feats of the English in connection with the Diamond Rock, which are described in the following pages, accusing Commodore Hood of exaggerating his prowess in order to mislead the London newspapers.

Like Martinique the Diamond Rock is of volcanic formation. Indeed, Captain Thomas Southey, R.N., in his Chronological History of the West Indies, in the compilation of which, it is said, he received the assistance of his brother the poet, records that in 1812: "About the middle of May, the Diamond Rock, off Martinico, threw up vast quantities of the same kind of calcined earths which issued in such abundance from the Souffrier [Soufrière] at St. Vincent's." In the absence, however, of any other reference to such an eruption, one is forced to the conclusion that Southey was either misled, or that he had in his mind an eruption of the Montagne Pelée in Martinique which occurred in that year.

Regarding the geological formation of the rock de Jonnès states: " The lava which forms the massif of this rock is a violet-brown porphyry, of a very fine formation, like that of petro-silex, which differs little from that of the Gros Morne (on the mainland), and I found the identical formation at the other extremity of the island, 20 leagues away, among the products of the oldest eruptions of the volcano of the Montagne Pelée." *

From 1794, when the island was captured by Sir John Jervis and Sir George Grey, until 1802 Martinique —or Martinico it was then called—was the head-quarters of the British forces in the West Indies. In the latter year it was restored to France by the Treaty of Amiens, and the harbour of Fort Royal—now Fort de France—from which de Grasse had sailed twenty years earlier to meet defeat in the Battle of the Saints, became the base of France's naval operations in the Caribbean.

When, therefore, war again broke out in 1803, Martinique, now a French island, naturally became the objective of the British fleet, which in that year was under the command of Samuel Hood, a cousin of the admiral of the same name—afterwards Lord Hood— who captured the anchorage of Basseterre, St. Kitts, in 1782. Commodore Hood had already seen much service in the West Indies. In 1802 he was appointed one of the Commissioners for the Government of Trinidad with Fullarton and Picton, the future hero of the

* " Aventures de la Guèrre," p. 432.

THE HISTORIC DIAMOND ROCK

Peninsular, and he succeeded Rear-Admiral Totty as the "Commodore and Commander-in-Chief of His Majesty's Ships and Vessels employed in the Windward and Leeward Charibbee Islands," hoisting his broad pennant on board the *Centaur*. On the renewal of war he captured St. Lucia and Tobago, as well as Demerara, Essequibo and Berbice, the colonies on the mainland of South America which now constitute British Guiana.

Under this distinguished officer a rigid blockade of Fort Royal was established; but its efficacy was greatly reduced through the French vessels being able to elude their pursuers by dodging behind the Diamond Rock, a circumstance which proved a source of considerable annoyance to Hood. He was not to be beaten, however, by what seemed to him to be such a trifling matter, and before the close of the year 1803 he conceived the brilliant idea of fortifying the rock (which he considered a "perfect naval post," and one which thirty riflemen could keep against ten thousand) and of harassing the enemy's ships from its precipitous sides.

Hood accordingly took possession of the rock early in January 1804, and entrusted the arrangement of works of defence and batteries upon it to James Wilkes Maurice, first of his flagship the *Centaur*, a dashing young officer who had already greatly distinguished himself on the occasion of the capture of St. Lucia, Tobago, and the Dutch colonies on the mainland. Maurice had also earned the gratitude of his commander by a brilliant and highly successful attack on a fort in Martinique in the preceding year. Early one morning, as the *Centaur* was passing Cape de Salines, she was fired at from a fort, and several shots were exchanged. A party of marines under Captain Crozier, and forty seamen under Maurice and Lieutenant Ayscough were therefore landed at Anse d'Arlet to destroy the fort. On the first alarm the national guards assembled and came to the assistance of the fourteen gunners stationed in the battery, but they had not time to arrange themselves in defence of the narrow and steep path which led to an eminence on which a brass 2-pounder was mounted before the English were upon them and put them to flight. Only one man was captured, the remainder fleeing precipitately to the woods. The battery, mounting six 24-pounders, was completely destroyed, and the guns, etc., thrown over the precipice ; but unfortunately, owing to the premature explosion of the magazine, one British seaman was killed, and Lieutenant Maurice, Captain Crozier and Lieutenant Walker, R.N., with six men were wounded. For their gallantry on this occasion Maurice and Ayscough were each presented with a sword of the value of £50, by the Patriotic Fund.

To return to the Diamond Rock. Measured by quadrant from the deck of the *Ulysses*, the height of the rock was found to be 600 feet, while its circumference was estimated at about a mile. The south side, which runs like a wall sheer down into the water, proved inaccessible, and so, too, did the east and south-west sides, which are hollowed out into caves of immense size. Maurice and his small party, which consisted of one hundred and twenty men and boys, were, however, able to effect a landing on the west side among the breakers, which run there far out into the sea. From this point they crept on all-fours through crannies in the rocks until the north-west front was reached. Here they found a slope of green fig trees, which ended under a huge overhanging grotto, and it was on this favoured spot, which he called Portland Place, that the "Governor" pitched his tent.

Three 24-pounders and two 18-pounders were then mounted on the rock—a proceeding which was only carried out with the greatest difficulty. "Lieutenant Maurice, having succeeded in scrambling up the side of the rock (rarely, perhaps never before, trodden by man), and fastened one end of an 8-inch hawser to a pinnacle, the viol-block was converted into a traveller, with a purchase-block lashed thereto, and the other end of the hawser set up as a jack-stay, round the *Centaur's* mainmast. The gun being slung to the viol, the purchase-fall was brought to the capstern. In this manner the desired object was effected in a week, during which time Lieutenant Maurice and the working party on shore suffered most dreadfully from excessive heat and fatigue, being constantly exposed to the sun, and frequently obliged to lower themselves down over immense precipices to attend the ascent of the guns, and bear them off from the innumerable projections against which they swung whenever the ship took a shear, which often occurred and caused considerable delay." *

"Were you to see," wrote Mr. J. Eckstein, to whom Commodore Hood gave permission to live on the rock to make drawings, "how, along a dire, and, I had almost said, a perpendicular acclivity, the sailors are hanging in clusters, hauling up a four-and-twenty pounder by hawsers, you would wonder! They appear like mice, hauling a little sausage; scarcely can we hear the Governor on the top, directing them with his trumpet, the *Centaur* lying close under it, like a cocoa-shell."

A four months' supply of provisions and water was put ashore and, as soon as the guns had been landed, active preparations were made for the defence of the position. On the lower part of the slope referred to above, a 24-pounder was mounted on a central point carriage. This formed the "Queen's Battery," which commanded the approach to the rock and also nearly the entire bay, across which no vessel could any longer pass unmolested. Here on January 19, Queen Charlotte's birthday, the British flag was hoisted, and a royal salute of twenty-one guns broke the stillness of the air, and here too the morning and evening guns were regularly fired. From the Queen's a covered way led to another Battery called after the flagship the Centaur, which faced the north-east. Here also a 24-pounder was mounted

* "Royal Naval Biography," Supplement Part I., by John Marshall, 1827.

130

HAULING CANNON UP THE ROCK FROM H.M.S. CENTAUR

THE NORTH-EAST FACE, SHOWING THE QUEEN'S BATTERY

THE DIAMOND ROCK
From engravings after the paintings by John Eckstein

and this commanded the sea on the other side. From these batteries the middle of the rock and Hood's Battery, which carried the third 24-pounder, were reached by means of a rope ladder, and from there the tortuous ascent to the top wound through shrubs and crags. On the very summit were the two 18-pounders from H.M.S. *Hippomenes*, over which for many a month the Union Jack proudly floated.

De Jonnès who, with spy-glass to his eye, was an interested spectator, watching the proceedings from the shores of Martinique, gives some additional information regarding the fortification of the rock.* He tells us that the disembarkation of the English sailors was facilitated by a timber keel which served as a landing stage. Above was a great break in the rock which was made still larger by mining. Here a kind of redoubt was made which was only accessible by a steep slope and was intended to be the last refuge of the garrison in case of emergency. On the lower level de Jonnès saw two circular batteries armed with 24-pounders. Entrenchments protected the entrance of several caves near by which could only be entered by narrow paths on the side of the rock. Here the barracks and provision stores were located. "The only path which led to the top of the rock ended in an immense cave, intersected by a platform on which a gun of large calibre, which covered the approaches, was mounted. Rope ladders fixed to iron staples enabled the sailors to reach the summit of the Diamond. . . ."

* " Aventures de la Guèrre," p. 433.

131

On the topmost point " there was a signal mast and, remarkable though it may seem, two 18-pounders to support it. To hoist them to so great a height was a feat of strength wonderfully conceived and very difficult of execution. The commodore succeeded in carrying it out by bringing his vessel so near the rock as almost to touch it on the leeward side. He then fixed grapnels and boarding anchors in cavities of the rock at different heights, and by means of this support and by tackle and winding tackle the guns were hoisted to the summit."

The sailors slung their hammocks in caves and tents, and so greatly did they enjoy their life on the Diamond that, in spite of the absence of their usual comforts and allowances, it was only with the greatest reluctance that they returned to their ships when occasion arose. There were springs on the rock, but they partook of a mineral character and the men were, consequently, almost entirely dependent on supplies of water from the ship. The *Centaur* was anchored quite close by over a patch of coral and soft rock about a mile distant bearing W. by N. ¾ N., and the commodore, who showed great activity and vigilance, visited the rock nearly every day. Provisions were landed in a bucket fixed to a pulley-block and ropes, an arrangement which the seamen nicknamed the Mail or Telegraph, and this also formed the means of communication for those of the men who were too nervous to trust themselves to the rope ladders.

Within six weeks of the landing, the Diamond

became a perfect hive of industry. Carpenters, smiths, turners and miners plied their respective trades with a will. With lime from St. Lucia and rude bricks blasted from the rock, a hospital was built, but there proved, happily, to be little use for it, so perfect was the health of the sailors in their new surroundings. With that remarkable ingenuity which is still so characteristic of our blue-jackets, anvils were fashioned out of old anchors, and from daybreak to dusk the rock resounded with the ring of hammers and the roar of forges.

For the first few months, time passed pleasantly enough. The place was healthy, the climate bracing and enjoyable and the scenery enchanting, while a goodly supply of madeira provided by the thoughtful Commodore Hood—to whom the rock became a perfect hobby—added not a little to the amenities of life. Indeed, the only serious drawbacks seem to have been the occasional scarcity of water, which was experienced when the *Centaur* left her anchorage, the presence of innumerable snakes, some of which were very poisonous, and the sharpness of the rocks, which made it extremely difficult for the men to get about. Animal life on the rock was represented by goats, rabbits, tropical birds and doves, and also by Captain Maurice's pets—a Newfoundland dog, a cat and a kitten—which he brought ashore with him from his ship.

Mr. Eckstein, the amateur historian of the rock, to whom reference has already been made, has left a glowing account of life upon it in a letter which is

published in the "Naval Chronicle".* " The rocks are so
bold and grand," he wrote, "that I feel inexpressible
delight in beholding them ; and then the wide seas,
with uncommon wild clouds flying about—I recognise
in my soul a feeling of relationship to the majesty of
Nature. The surge often drives the spray as high as I
sit ; it is a music of which the ear never tires. I mess
with Captain Morris [Maurice], and we generally have
visitors ; the link of good nature is never broken, and
we are as profusely liberal as our circumstances and
situation will admit. Each lends the other his spoon,
a penknife serves to cut up a joint, and fingers are a
substitute for forks. The language of the heart flows
here as purely as at the proudest board of ticklish
taste ; it is unadulterated from the source of Nature.
A bottle of madeira or claret follows dinner, to the
remembrance of our friends in England. Fish, melons,
etc., are sometimes brought from the Martinique shores
by the small boats which venture here for gain or
curiosity. We throw the shot upon their shore, and
bring every boat to if we please. In the evening we
walk in the Queen's Battery, thus tracing our rocky
path along the over-hanging ridge, to the summit,
where our little brotherly tents spread their canvas on
cross-sticks, and are barricaded with stones. Warmed
by the genial bowl, we shake hands, bid good-night,
retire upon the dried grass, and, rolled in blankets,
sleep shuts our weary eyelids, while neither fear nor
uneasiness intrudes on our repose. At night the

* The " Naval Chronicle ", London, 1804, Vol. 12, p. 208.

THE "MAIL COACH" AND ALTERNATIVE LADDERS

THE "CURIEUX" BROUGHT AS A PRIZE TO THE ROCK

THE DIAMOND ROCK

From engravings after the paintings by John Eckstein

continual roaring of the sea below is only interrupted by the replies of watching sentinels above, or the screams of the tropic bird, who sweeps from the top to the water to catch fish, which he providently lays up in his nest to feed on by day. If then, sometimes, the thought of those distant beings, dear to affection, keep my sense awake, I behold the starry face of the heavens as I lean on my elbow, the sea stretching before me her immeasurable blue domain, and, trusting to the wakeful eye of Providence, I sink in reflection, thought dissolves, and oblivion removes every trace from the tablet of memory."

Discipline on the rock was rigidly enforced, and any familiarity which a Robinson Crusoe-like existence might be calculated to engender between officers and seamen was sternly repressed. Acting-Lieutenant Roger Woolcombe, for example, was court-martialled for his " unofficer-like conduct in messing at the top of the rock with a part of the crew," a charge which was proved, and led to the lieutenant being reprimanded.

Rigid sanitary regulations were adopted with the object of safeguarding the health of the crew. With yellow fever periodically ravaging the islands and decimating the white inhabitants it is not surprising that the well-being of the seamen, destined to spend weeks within a circumscribed area without, of course, any sanitary appliances or water supply, was a constant cause of anxiety. The carrying out of these rules seems, however, to have been left largely to the good sense of the men themselves, the chief penalty inflicted on those who transgressed being a liberal measure of ridicule. The author has seen it recorded—where, he cannot recollect—that if any man was found relieving nature in a place not set apart for the purpose he was compelled to carry a broom until he found some other individual committing a similar offence. Then and then only could he relinquish it to the latest offender.

A constant watch was kept for the enemy, and not a vessel flying the French colours was suffered to pass without receiving attentions of a decidedly disagreeable nature from one or more of the batteries on the Diamond Rock. When the alarm was given, every man would be at his post within five minutes, and the small garrison was brought by its gallant commander to a very high state of efficiency.

Having garrisoned the rock and landed an adequate supply of victuals for the sustenance of its "crew," Commodore Hood sailed in the *Centaur* to Antigua to refit in English Harbour there. The remainder of the ships of his squadron also left for St. Lucia, there being less immediate need for them now that the rock was fortified. While the coast was thus more or less clear an attack was made on the Diamond, in which Moreau de Jonnès,* who has been quoted more than once in the preceding pages, himself took a prominent part. It resulted, however, in complete failure, and nearly ended disastrously to the invading party as the following pages will show.

On May 3, 1804, which he, with some reason, called a "jour de malheur," a certain Colonel Miany came to

* "Aventures de la Guèrre," p. 435 *et seq.*

him in a state of great agitation, with the information that the Captain General Villaret Joyeuse had put him in charge of an expedition which was to carry the Diamond Rock by assault in the night. Villaret Joyeuse believed that it would be possible for four old and heavy harbour boats to master the rapid currents of the St. Lucia Channel, and, in spite of the surf, for forty soldiers to land from them on a small ledge of rock. De Jonnès was selected to accompany the colonel, on account of his knowledge of the route to be traversed, and of the defensive works which had been carried out by the English.

From the first de Jonnès despaired of success, believing that some evil spirit must have shaken the sound judgment of the admiral in planning such an expedition. Then Miany remembered that at the interview which he had had with the Captain General "a miserable little red-faced man" was present, whom he had at once recognised as being an officer who had been in the service of the English in 1794, and, when Martinique was attacked by Admiral Jervis and Sir Charles Grey, effectively contributed towards bringing about Rochambeau's capitulation by suggesting the attack on Fort Royal instead of Fort Bourbon, a proceeding which compelled the French general to surrender two days later. In other words, Miany recognised the "little red-faced man" as a traitor, who had once already been rewarded for his services by the English and was now again in the service of France.

When de Jonnès heard this, he made up his mind that the expedition about to be undertaken had been sold to the enemy; but it was too late to urge any alteration in the plans. Only an hour remained in which to make the preparations. Miany spent half the time with his notary and with his confessor. De Jonnès collected all his worldly goods in an apron and entrusted them to a family, which he left in tears, praying God for his safety.

When he arrived at the head of the harbour, where the troops were to be embarked he found that the "secret" expedition was known to all and sundry, most of the inhabitants of the town having turned out to witness its departure. The white people protested that the men were being sent off to certain butchery, and that the author of the undertaking must be either a traitor or an idiot. The coloured women on the other hand were sobbing, and for long after the members of the expedition left the wharf they could hear their cries and benedictions, which no doubt did not help to encourage them.

Captain Halgan, who was in charge of the naval side of the undertaking, declared that the Captain General himself had come to the harbour, but that, hearing that he was likely to meet with a hostile reception by the indignant inhabitants, he had withdrawn.

It had been hoped that it would be possible to make the attack on the rock at daybreak, but by three in the morning only half of the distance to it had been traversed, and as that was over the quiet waters of the bay of Fort de France it could not really be considered as much as that. The flotilla was, moreover, delayed by one boat having to wait for another, and soon,

138

therefore, the order of progression in line ahead was abandoned.

When the boats reached the Anse Mathurin, by the Islet aux Ramiers or Pigeon Island, a rest was decided upon. The sailors, who were already weary, landed, and de Jonnès commandeered some provisions for them from the officers in charge of the fort there, a proceeding which became necessary as a boat which was loaded with bread and wine had fallen behind and could not rejoin the others until the next day. He hailed an old comrade of his named Parmentier, who was in charge of a fort 120 feet above, and that individual let down three ladders and joined the expedition; de Jonnès persuading him to enter the first boat and to accompany the party.

Long before daybreak on the following morning the boats were again under way. The voyage now became more perilous. The boats had to pick their way along at the foot of the steep cliffs, against the base of which the waves dashed thundering into the caves which they had hollowed out. The night was clear and from the Islet aux Ramiers the expedition for a time made good progress, although they had to double five promontories, which could only be rounded by risking the boats in the waters of the open sea. They rowed for ten or twelve leagues in this manner, and at about three in the morning reached the Petite Anse du Diamant, which is shut in on one side by the slopes of the Morne la Croix and on the other by those of the Gros Morne.

Behind the latter the Diamond Rock could be seen,

dark and threatening. To de Jonnès it appeared to be
" as inaccessible as the wonderful peaks which Sinbad
the Sailor vainly tried to approach in the Indian
Ocean, and from which malevolent and supernatural
powers repelled him."

On the shores of this small bay the men again
landed in order to secure much needed repose, and
de Jonnès took the opportunity of sending Parmentier
with a sergeant up the hillside to the Gros Morne to
see if perchance any traitors were signalling their
approach to the English on the Diamond. Once ashore
the fatigued sailors were regaled with coffee, " being
in the country of the finest coffee in the world, not
even excepting Moka."

Darkness being essential to the success of the rash
expedition it was not until two in the morning that the
boats were again shoved off. Then the troubles began.
Once out of the shelter of the bay the boats were
pitched and tossed about in a ruthless manner by the
heavy swell which prevailed. As long as they were
coasting under the cliffs there was no imminent danger,
only their progress being delayed. When, however,
they reached the point and felt the full force of the
current which races through the St. Lucia Channel
matters became serious. Although there was no wind
the sea was rough, and the boats were thrown and
dashed about as if they were on a reef.

They were now in the deep channel separating the
Diamond from the Gros Morne. By desperate efforts
half the distance was traversed, and hopes that the
rock would be reached were already running high

when the fleet of boats was broken up into disorder by the fury of the waves.

"All right," cried Miany, who was in the foremost boat, "we will attack the rock alone! Forward!" No sooner were these words out of his mouth than the boat, pulled by six steady rowers, was swept away like a cork—"as a little boat would be by the flood waters of the Loire or the Seine." Consternation prevailed, but no one gave a thought to the danger of the situation. What overwhelmed them was the knowledge that this misfortune had occurred just as they were reaching the enemy, for they were now so near that they could distinguish the glow of the lanterns in the batteries on the rock.

The din of the surf was deafening and its violence so great that neither boat nor cutter could have lain alongside the sill of rock upon which the men were to have been disembarked. Had they attempted to do so they would inevitably have been dashed to pieces.

Though the men were now soaked to the skin they were still in no imminent danger, but the force of the current was carrying the boats out into the open sea, and when the second day after their departure broke de Jonnès estimated that they had drifted at least six leagues out of their course. They were soon, however, carried across the current into smooth water.

When the sun rose those in the foremost boat could see all but one of the others—mere specks on the horizon. Through the glass they noticed that the decks were swept clean, sails were gone, and the rowers exhausted. One boat was missing, and to add to the peril of the situation there was the fear always present that an English cruiser might at any moment put in an appearance. Still, Bengal lights were burnt and the sight of these greatly encouraged the sailors who, after desperate efforts, managed to join forces with their comrades once again.

Discouraged and disheartened the flotilla at last succeeded in regaining the peaceful waters of the Anse d'Arlet. The sailors were now quite worn out, and so stiff through cold and exposure that they could scarcely rise from their seats. Some of the men were indeed so exhausted that it was not until their limbs had been chafed and rubbed with rum that their vitality was restored.

Meanwhile, what had happened to Parmentier who was left making his way to the Gros Morne to look for spies? Accompanied by a sergeant he reached, by a narrow path at the foot of the Gros Morne, a position immediately opposite the Diamond Rock. Here regardless of the danger from snakes, the two hid under a bundle of dead leaves. What then occurred shall be given in de Jonnès own words. " At eleven o'clock they heard the voices and footfall of two men who were cutting their way through the forest, and passed quite near them : one was a negro and the other an English sailor. As soon as they reached the platform they struck a light, lit a candle and prepared to light with it a signal-lantern which they had brought with them, which would show a red colour. They had not time, however, to carry out their plan. Attacked by the two artillerymen they were killed on the spot without being able to make use of their arms. . . . It was evident that if these men had made their signal to the garrison of the Diamond our boats would, when they were about two hundred fathoms from their batteries, have been over-whelmed, and not one of us would have survived to tell of the ambuscade in which we had perished. We were all in a state of great indignation and rage caused by this discovery, when the arrival of a despatch-boat containing a stranger was reported to the colonel. Our force was put in a military posture, and the boat was captured and the officer who was in it compelled to make known his identity. It was the promoter of our expedition. As soon as he recognised him Miany turned purple with rage, and without listening to his explanation that he was a messenger from the admiral sent to find out how we were getting on he apostrophised him . . . then, snatching the sword which I had in my hand, he threw himself upon his adversary, calling upon him to put himself on guard. Miany made a plunge at him at the same moment, and without engaging swords struck him a blow on the wrist which disarmed him, and another on the head which would have cracked his skull if he had not leaped aside as he did with such precipitation that he fell his whole length on the ground ten paces way. The colonel made desperate efforts to recommence the fight, but while Halgan held him back I led the unfortunate paladin to his canoe, advising him to tell the admiral that he had not met us, and adding that if he valued his life he would take care not to cross the path of the colonel."

To return to de Jonnés and his party. The spirits of the men were soon raised by the arrival of an American whaler bringing their twenty-five comrades from the boat which they supposed to have been lost, and soon afterwards the party returned across the mountains to Fort de France. The expedition had signally failed.

Of the many brilliant deeds performed in the neighbourhood of Diamond Rock at this period, none stands out more prominently than the capture of the French corvette, *Curieux*, on February 4, 1805. This vessel, which was equipped with sixteen long French 6-pounders and had on board one hundred men, was the pride of Martinique, and the favourite ship of Admiral Villaret Joyeuse, the Captain General of the island. She had been sent out from the Careenage to a position under Fort Edward, and Lieutenant Robert Carthew Reynolds, with Lieutenant Bettesworth and Mr. Tracey of the *Centaur*, volunteered to cut her out. Their offer was accepted, and accordingly on the first dark night they set off in four boats, with a party of sixty seamen and twelve marines, to accomplish their purpose.

After a stiff pull of twenty miles, with muffled oars, they reached the corvette and caught the crew napping. Though her boarding nettings were out, a rope ladder hung over the stern, and up this Lieutenant Reynolds sprang, closely followed by Richard Templeman, an able seaman, who hacked away the netting with his cutlass as he gained the deck. This enabled the men in the three remaining boats to board the vessel on the quarter. The moon was just rising, when six sentries, posted in the

Curieux, hurriedly gave the alarm. The French officers were on deck in a trice, and lining up across it offered a staunch resistance to the boarders. A desperate encounter ensued, during which the Frenchmen behaved with great bravery; but every one of them was soon wounded, and while some were thrown down the hatchway others retreated to the fo'c'sle, where the sailors were gathered together armed with pikes. The boarding party, however, succeeded in hacking their way to the cables, which were speedily severed, and it was not long before the *Curieux* was triumphantly brought a prize to Diamond Rock, where the victors received an ovation from the garrison.

The British loss in this engagement was three officers and six seamen wounded, while of the French no fewer than forty were killed or wounded. Captain Cordier, of the *Curieux*, had a remarkable escape; he was thrown from his vessel, but being caught by the flukes of the anchor, slipped into a boat, and was subsequently rowed ashore in an unconscious condition by one of his seamen.

Lieutenant Reynolds, in recognition of his gallant conduct, was given command of the prize, which now became one of his Majesty's sloops of war; but he did not live long to enjoy the honour. In the September following he died of his wounds, and his remains were deposited on Diamond Rock, where, it is to be assumed, they still lie. The funeral of this brave and popular officer was conducted with as much ceremony as circumstances would allow. All the officers of the *Centaur*, and every man and boy in the ship who had witnessed his brilliant exploit attended; and Captain Maurice was himself one of the chief mourners.

With regard to Bettesworth, who shared with Reynolds the honours for the successful cutting-out of the *Curieux*, Southey records that the career of that officer was short and brilliant. It seems that he succeeded to the command of the *Curieux*, and, on one occasion, when he was cruising in her off the Spanish Main, he went for a row in his jolly boat, taking with him the purser, who beguiled the time by playing the Marseillaise upon a violin. A treacherous negro enticed him to land by offering fowls for sale. Bettesworth pulled ashore, and was at once attacked by a squadron of cavalry. He was wounded in the thigh, and his coxswain had his arm broken by another shot. The rest of the seamen lay down in the boat, and would inevitably have been all taken, if Bettesworth had not stimulated them with reproaches, and urged them to shove the boat off, which they then did.

When clear, Bettesworth, exhausted from loss of blood, reminded the purser that there was a bottle of champagne in the boat, and asked him to draw the cork and give some to him and the wounded men. Southey relates : " The purser's nerves were out of tune, and in attempting to draw the cork he knocked the bottom off the bottle, and the invaluable refreshment was lost. The purser determined never to play the Marseillaise hymn again."

To Bettesworth fell the honour of conveying to England Nelson's despatches from Antigua, apprising the Government of Villeneuve's homeward flight, a

service for which he was immediately promoted, by
Lord Barham, to be post-captain. He was subsequently
appointed to the command of H.M.S. *Tartar*, and
met his end, at the early age of twenty-three, in an
engagement off Bergen. He married a daughter of the
first Earl Grey, and his widow married Mr. Edward
Ellice, the Whig politician. It is recorded that Nelson
stated that Bettesworth was the only officer in the navy
who had more wounds than himself.

To return to the rock. Up to the end of 1804 no
serious efforts had been made to dislodge the British
from their eyrie, and it was not until May in the
following year, 1805, that their position became to
any extent insecure. On the 16th of that month, at
half-past seven in the morning, the watch spied a large
vessel rounding Point de Salines. From her general
appearance and from the cut of her jib, it became clear
that she was one of the enemy. Half an hour later the
Spanish ensign and pennant fluttered from her peak.
Captain Maurice at once ordered the French colours to
be hoisted on the rock, and this stratagem served its
purpose, for the vessel proceeded on her way, and at
twenty minutes to nine came under the lee of the rock
at a distance of three-quarters of a mile. The French
flag was then replaced by the British colours, and a
well-directed fire of round shot and grape was opened on
her. The first shot struck the vessel under the fore
channels. She immediately put up her helm, and in the
act of wearing returned one feeble shot. The wind
being light, however, it was not until nine that she got
out of range, and she continued running before the wind

147

until twelve. At two, an enemy's brig stood out of Fort Royal and beat to windward of the rock off which she still cruised.

Captain Maurice was now satisfied that a general attack was contemplated, and he was not wrong, for from the 16th to 29th the rock was completely blockaded by frigates, brigs, schooners and small sloop-rigged boats, detached from Admiral Villeneuve's fleet, which had just reached the West Indies little knowing that they were being hotly pursued by Nelson. They effectively prevented any supplies from reaching the garrison: and on the 25th a sloop from St. Lucia containing the second lieutenant, Roger Woolcombe, who had carried despatches to Barbados, and the purser with a four months' supply of provisions, was captured as they were endeavouring to throw in some barrels of powder although she was covered by a spirited fire from the Fort Diamond, Centaur's Battery and Maurice's Battery.

Just before sundown on the 29th a squadron commanded by Commodore Cosmao consisting of two seventy-fours, the *Pluton* and the *Berwick*; the 36-gun frigate *Sirène*; the 16-gun brig corvette *Argus* with eleven gunboats in tow, each mounting three pieces of cannon, set out from Fort Royal under all sail, having on board 300 to 400 troops of the line commanded by Chef d'Escadron Boyer. On the 30th at sunrise the enemy had fallen far to leeward; but the wind veering very much to the southward enabled them to fetch a bay where they continued under easy sail for the night. Daybreak on the 31st found them

148

still proceeding under easy sail and well to windward, but at 7 they bore down on the rock with all haste.

Recognising the impossibility of defending the lower works against such a force, Captain Maurice reluctantly gave orders for them to be abandoned, and after spiking two of his guns, drowning the powder and cutting away the launch, the defenders, with the exception of the cook who was afterwards taken prisoner retired to the higher defences of the rock by what was known as the North Garden Pass. At ten minutes to eight every man had withdrawn and the ladders were secured not a moment too soon, for the *Berwick* had already opened fire within pistol shot, and at eight the whole squadron was in action, its fire being hotly returned by the 24-pounder in Hood's Battery halfway up the rock and two 18-pounders in the Fort Diamond.

Captain Maurice now busied himself with the placing of his men on the different lodgments with small arms to harass the enemy when they landed, and the execution which our sailors did with their muskets was considerable. Indeed, their fire was so galling that the French only dared to leave three seamen in each of the boats, and even these men were soon shot dead. Three of the gunboats went adrift; two ran ashore on Martinique and were beaten to pieces, and the others drifted out to sea. Throughout the day the entire squadron continued vigorously to bombard the rock, and night found the whole of the small force of defenders at their posts in desperate straits,

149

but still prepared to harass the enemy as they threw in supplies and reinforcements. The bombardment continued without ceasing on June 1 and 2, when the enemy were reinforced by another brig. The fire from the rock was galling; but the enemy effected a landing during the night of the 1st, and finding shelter under the overhanging and surf-beaten rocks fired at each Englishman who ventured to show himself. Chef d'Escadron Boyer thought that the crags would be easy to climb, but he was soon disillusioned, finding nothing but immense precipices, perpendicular rocks and a threatening enemy before him. The French suffered severely from the musketry fire and from fragments of rock, cannon-balls and casks full of stones which were hurled down upon them, and the landing party were cut off from their supports and provisions.

On the evening of the 2nd Boyer decided at once to call upon the garrison to surrender, but, after examining the rock above the cavern where he was sheltering, it occurred to him that it might, after all, be possible to scale it and make his victory more decisive. He accordingly sent for scaling ladders and gave orders to a captain, a lieutenant and sixty grenadiers to prepare for an attack in the morning. At nine a number of men who had been reconnoitring the position returned with the news that they had found various ways of getting up the rock, and an hour later Captain Cortes reached a height which commanded the defenceless position. He was followed by Lieutenant Girandon and a party of grenadiers, marines and soldiers. But

at four in the afternoon Captain Maurice had found
that he had little powder left and not enough ball
cartridges to last till dark ; and " being firmly of the
opinion the enemy meant to carry the heights by
assault that night," he thought that it was a duty
which he owed to his brave men who had supported
him so gallantly during three days and two nights'
constant battle to offer terms of capitulation. So,
after consultation with his first lieutenant Mr. R. A.
Wadham, he threw out a flag of truce at 4.30, "the
unhappiest moment of my life," as he wrote afterwards
in his despatch to Rear-Admiral Cochrane. At five
the reply was received, Boyer being thus deprived of
his final triumph, and honourable terms were conceded
to the gallant defenders.

Next morning they embarked on the *Pluton* and the
Berwick, and on June 4 all—with the exception of
fourteen men who were detained on the ground that
they were French—were sent to Barbados, and the
French flag replaced the Union Jack which for eighteen
months had braved the battle and the breeze on
Diamond Rock.

During the siege the sufferings of the garrison were
intense, and the fatigue and hardship to which they
were subjected were aggravated by the almost total
lack of water. A tank capable of holding 500 tons
had been constructed in a ravine ; but unfortunately
it proved useless as no rain whatever fell while the rock
was occupied. Day after day, and night after night,
the men had not a moment's rest, and inasmuch as only
one pint of water was made to last 24 hours it is

151

not to be wondered at that many fainted and were otherwise incapacitated.

On arriving at Barbados, Captain Maurice reported the surrender of the rock to Lord Nelson, who had reached Carlisle Bay in pursuit of Villeneuve two days before, in a letter couched in the following terms :—

"BARBADOES, *6th June*, 1805.

" MY LORD,

"It is with the greatest sorrow I have to inform you of the loss of the Diamond Rock under my command, which was obliged to surrender on the 2nd instant, after three days' attack from a squadron of two sail of the line, one frigate, one brig, a schooner, eleven gunboats, and, from the nearest calculation, 1500 troops. The want of ammunition and water was the sole occasion of this unfortunate loss. Although I shall never cease to regret the accident, yet it is some consolation to think so many valuable lives are saved to His Majesty's service, having only two killed and one wounded. The enemy, from the nearest account I have been able to obtain, lost on shore thirty killed and forty wounded, independent of the ships and boats : they also lost three gun-boats and two rowing-boats. Allow me to speak in the highest terms of the officers and men under my command, and I trust, when the court-martial shall have taken place, that their hardships, fatigue, and gallantry will merit your lord-ship's approbation, they having been nineteen nights under arms, and some of them obliged to drink their own

152

water. I beg leave to enclose the articles of capitulation.

"I have the honour to remain, &c.,

"J. W. MAURICE.

"To the Right Hon. Viscount Nelson, &c. &c."

The articles of capitulation were as follows:

"Article I. That the rock, with all its works, shall be delivered up entire.

"II. That the garrison shall be allowed to march to the Queen's Battery with drums beating and colours flying, and there lay down their arms.

"III. That all private property shall be secured to the officers and men.

"IV. That the garrison shall be sent to Barbadoes, at the expense of the French Nation; but not to serve till regularly exchanged.

"V. That the garrison is capable of holding out a few days longer, and two hours are given for an answer, when hostilities will be recommenced.

"J. W. MAURICE."

Lord Nelson's acknowledgment, which was dated " *Victory* at Sea, June 8th, 1805," was generous, and must have been very gratifying to the brave little band of defenders. It ran as follows:—

"*Victory* at Sea, *June 8th*, 1805.

"SIR,

"I have received your letter of the 6th instant. acquainting me with the surrender of the Diamond

153

Rock under your command, on the 2nd of this month, to a squadron of the enemy's ships and gunboats therein mentioned, together with the terms of capitulation which accompanied your said letter. In answer to which, while I regret the loss of the Diamond, I have no doubt that every exertion has been used by yourself, and those under your command for its defence, and that its surrender has been occasioned from the circumstances you represent. It is particularly gratifying that so few lives were lost in the contest, and I have very fully to express my approbation of the terms of capitulation, as well as with your conduct personally, and that of the officers and men under your command, which I have to request you will be pleased to communicate to them.

"I am, Sir,

"Your most obedient humble servant,

"NELSON AND BRONTE."

The usual court-martial followed, but it was only a formal affair. It met on board H.M.S. *Circe* in Carlisle Bay, Barbados, on June 24, 1805, in pursuance of an order of the Hon. Rear-Admiral Cochrane, who succeeded Commodore Hood in command of the Leeward Islands station. Captain Jonas Rose of the *Circe* presided, and the Court comprised William Champion, George Tobin, Joseph Nourse and Robert Henderson, with Thomas Hort as Deputy Judge Advocate.

As soon as the proceedings had been opened, a lengthy letter was read from Captain Maurice, detailing the circumstances which led to the surrender of the

154

rock, and after hearing this the Court at once expressed opinion that "he, the Officers and Company of His Majesty's late sloop Diamond Rock, did everything in their power to the very last, in the defence of the rock, and against a most superior force; and Captain James W. Maurice behaved with firm and determined resolu_ tion, and did not surrender the Diamond until he was unable to make further defence for want of water and ammunition; the Court do therefore honourably acquit Captain Maurice accordingly." They added: "The Court cannot dismiss Captain James W. Maurice without expressing their admiration of his conduct in the whole of the occasion; and also they express the highest approbation of the support given by the officers and men under his command; a circumstance that does high honour to them; does no less credit and honour to the discipline by Captain J. W. Maurice; and therefore do unanimously and honourably acquit the said Officers and ship's Company, and they are unanimously and honourably acquitted accordingly."

The president expressed himself happy at it falling to his lot to return Captain Maurice his sword, which had been so honourably drawn in the service of his country, and addressing the defenders commended their conduct in the highest terms of approbation.

With Lieutenant Woolcombe and Mr. Ricardo, the purser, it was otherwise. Admiral Cochrane recommended that these two officers who had arrived in a cartel*

* A vessel employed for exchanging prisoners of war. It was unarmed, mounting one gun only for signalling purposes.

from Martinique should be tried by court-martial,
Captain Maurice having informed him that "the above
persons (for gentlemen I cannot call them)" had behaved
in a disgraceful manner. Being sent from St. Lucia
with ammunition for the garrison, they "tarried to
go aboard a transport and· get drunk." This it was
that led to their capture by the enemy.

As has already been hinted, the French professed to
consider the rock of no importance whatever, "till it
struck the fancy of Commodore Hood to sink millions
of money in it." The *Martinique Gazette* was lamentably flippant about the whole episode : "This rock,
qualified nevertheless by the British Gazettes with the
pompous appellation of 'The Gibraltar of the Windward Islands,' and with which the administration of that
country have been pleased to amuse the public by the
most exaggerated accounts and poetical descriptions,
was taken possession of by the French soldiers in three
days. Though this conquest will be considered but
trifling to our armies, accustomed to far greater
triumphs, it is not the less glorious to the handful of
brave men concerned in it. It will always be said to
their honour that 200 Frenchmen conquered in a few
hours a place that nature, art, and eighteen months'
incessant labour had conjoined to render in some degree
impregnable. It is true that it cost the English much
less trouble to occupy it, for nobody before Sir Samuel
Hood ventured to dispute the possession of it with the
reptiles and birds of the sea, which reigned there for ages
without a rival.

"It was a post thus fortified that the French soldiers

carried in sixty hours—had there been a French garrison upon it of 100 men, with provisions and ammunition, it would probably have held out against 10,000 men. But such is the fortune of the two belligerent nations, that the one has the superiority in money, as the other has it in bravery; and the result to the latter must be, that it will also have the money."

For this expression of opinion the *Barbados Mercury* of June 29, 1805, took its French contemporary to task: "To their bombast we do not look for Captain Maurice's panegyric, although we trace his valour in their difficulties and distress; from his own countrymen and brother officers, who best know how to discriminate the real hero, he has received the most honourable approval of his conduct; and on the close of the court-martial held on him for the surrender of the rock, the president expressed himself happy that it fell to his lot to return him his sword, which had been so honourably drawn in the cause of his country; and made no doubt, when his services were again called on, that they would be equally conspicuous. He then addressed the ship's company, and commended their conduct in the highest terms of approbation, for gallantry and discipline; and was confident that it would be an example in his Majesty's service."

Captain Maurice returned to England, where he, no doubt, received many congratulations upon the heroic defence of the Diamond Rock. Indeed, it is recorded that he was personally thanked by Lord Nelson, whom he was privileged to meet on board the *Victory* at Portsmouth very shortly before his departure for Gibraltar.

157

He was immediately appointed to the *Savage* brig, and after two years cruising in the Channel he once more went out—in that vessel—to the West Indies. In the autumn of 1808 Admiral Sir Alexander Cochrane appointed him governor of the West Indian island of Marie Galante, which he had captured from the French in the preceding March. Ill-health, however, compelled him to return to England in the following year. Then a further opportunity was given to this gallant officer of distinguishing himself, the Lords Commissioners of the Admiralty appointing him to be governor of the small island of Anholt in the Cattegat, which we had taken from the Danes in 1809, with a view to restoring the lighthouse upon it—a matter of considerable import-ance to the British men-of-war and merchantmen navigating the dangerous waters surrounding it. The island was also useful as a depôt and a point of communication with the mainland.

Here then Captain Maurice was stationed with a garrison of 350 marines and 31 men of the marine artillery, and here, curiously enough, he soon had an experience similar in many respects to that which he and his brave sailors underwent upon Diamond Rock.

For some time the Danes had been contemplating an attack upon the island, and operations with this object in view were begun in 1810. While, however, the sea remained open British ships of war patrolled the neigh-bourhood. This did not suit the plans of the Danes, who were again prevented from carrying on their offensive operations in the winter through the sea being frozen over.

THE DIAMOND ROCK

On March 23, however, in the following year, when the ice broke, a flotilla of twelve Danish gunboats, escorting twelve transports containing about 1000 men, reached Anholt and a vigorous siege ensued. Under cover of a fog the Danish troops were disembarked, Maurice and his men went out to meet them and a sharp engagement took place, which resulted in the complete defeat of the Danes, who fled precipitately, leaving behind 520 officers and men besides twenty-three wounded. Though it is only fair to say that the fortunes of the day were believed to have been turned by the arrival of his Majesty's ships *Tartar* and *Sheldrake*, of whose presence the Danes had been unaware, the honours rested with Maurice and his gallant men.

Maurice retained the governorship of Anholt until September, 1812, and this was the last active appointment which he held. He retired with the rank of rear-admiral on October 1, 1846, and on September 4, 1857, the hero of Diamond Rock died at Stonehouse in his eighty-third year.

After capturing the rock the French hurled the guns down the precipices into the sea, and set about to destroy the batteries with such energy that in a very short space of time few traces were left of the work carried out with so much industry by Maurice and his men. In a tropical climate bush grows rapidly, and it does not take long to obliterate the handiwork of man. It is probable that if one were to land on the Diamond he would find little or nothing upon it to remind him of the stirring events of 1804-5.

But the rock is hardly ever visited nowadays, though

159

fishermen from the villages of Martinique occasionally land upon it for the purpose of collecting the eggs of the sea birds which abound in its fastnesses. Diamond Rock is now forlorn and deserted ; but its glory can never fade.

Now, much has been written about this famous rock being commissioned as a sloop of war and figuring on the books of the Admiralty as " H.M.S. *Diamond Rock*," but the actual despatches certainly do not bear out these stories. It is true that in the log of the *Centaur* of February 4, 1804, the following entry appears :—

" Ordered the Diamond Rock to be put on the establishment of a Sloop of War for the more effectual blockade of Martinique and to annoy their trade."

Commodore Hood's despatch to the Secretary of the Admiralty regarding Maurice's appointment throws, however, an entirely different light on the appointment. It runs as follows :—

" *Centaur*, DIAMOND, OFF MARTINIQUE.
" *7th Feb.*, 1804.

" SIR,

" In the singular situation of the Diamond so close to the enemy's shore, and the indication the Captain General (Villaret Joyeuse) made of attack, I thought it right a superior command to a lieutenant should be held, and have in consequence of the very zealous conduct of Lieutenant Maurice, first of the *Centaur*, in arranging its works since the commencement of hostilities, given him an acting order as Commander

CAPTAIN JAMES WILKES MAURICE
COMMANDER OF THE DIAMOND ROCK
From an engraving after John Eckstein

and one hundred men for the present establishment of the *Fort Diamond* as a sloop of War, including the Rock, by which warrant officers will be useful for the security of the stores, &c., with a lieutenant to command the vessel when she might leave the Rock on any service; a purser will also very much facilitate the arrangement and the surgeon will superintend a small hospital for thirty men or if necessary a few more in any casualties of bad fevers from the ship, and which will allow me to do away totally with the hospital at Barbadoes which is not half so healthy. I hope their Lordships will approve this measure which will be executed with little expence and may save thousands to the Country independant of its utility in consequence to the enemy and protection of the trade passing this channel." Such is Hood's letter verbatim.

That Diamond Rock figures in Steel's unofficial Navy List of 1804 is admitted; but an endorsement by the Lords Commissioners of the Admiralty on the corner of Hood's despatch seems to place it beyond doubt that it was a vessel—probably one captured from the French —and not the actual rock which was commissioned. The terms of this endorsement are as follows :

" Their Lordships thought proper to order the vessel attached to the service of the Diamond Rock to be registered by the name of the *Diamond Rock* Sloop and that a commission to command her be sent out to Lieut. Maurice."

The point is further emphasised by the fact that it is recorded that on the occasion of the court-martial of two officers some time after the surrender of the rock, " the Court asked Captain Maurice if there was a sloop called the *Diamond Rock*, and if the people on the Diamond Rock belonged to her, and if they were victualled from her and were paid as belonging to her." To this inquiry Maurice replied " that it was so."

From this it would seem to be certain that the rock itself was no more officially recognised as H.M.S. *Diamond Rock* than Portsmouth is as H.M.S. *Victory*, Whale Island as the *Excellent*, Sheerness as the *Wildfire*, and so on; the sailors on duty at those places being rated on the books of the respective vessels in order to bring them under the terms of the Navy Discipline Act.

The error into which a succession of writers on the West Indies appear to have fallen in stating that the rock itself figured in the Navy List in no way detracts, however, from the romance attached to the Diamond Rock and from the glamour which must always surround it.

CHAPTER VII

"LA GRANGE"

Viewed from the deck of a passing steamer, Roseau, the sleepy little capital of Dominica, fairest of all the Leeward Islands, presents a tranquil appearance which, as yet, hardly reflects the growing prosperity of the island or the beauty of its interior. In the open roadstead a few trim sloops and schooners may lie at anchor, while two or three steamers discharging their cargoes add some life to the scene; but on shore little movement can be discerned, and it is not easy to picture to oneself a time when this now peaceful town was raked by the broadsides of a hostile fleet.

In Dominica, La Grange is still spoken of; but the name is now less closely associated in the minds of most inhabitants with Napoleon's general who bore it than with a critical period in the island's history. That period was in 1805, when Dominica was in imminent danger of falling into the hands of the French and was only saved by the presence of mind and determination of the Governor, Brigadier-General Prevost, and the efficiency of the small body of regular troops and militia under his command.

Twenty-seven years before, the garrison had capitulated to the Marquis de Bouillé, whose troops had, as we read, marched through the streets of Roseau, "in most regular and solemn order," the drums beating a slow march, and the French soldiers, "with small boughs and flowers in their hats by way of laurels, with assumed fierce countenances as they came by our small force, which they seemed to threaten with instant dissolution." Four years later the tables were turned, and by the treaty of Versailles, which followed Rodney's victory over de Grasse, the term of the French occupation was brought to a conclusion, and the inhabitants were so elated at the restoration of British rule that by force of numbers they broke the halliards and overthrew the flagstaff in their eagerness to hoist upon it the Union flag.

Great, then, was the consternation, early in 1805, when it became known that a French fleet which had been closely blockaded at Rochefort for two years had escaped, and having reached the Caribbean Sea was engaged in making marauding expeditions among the islands, crippling our trade and spreading terror among the inhabitants.

Defences were hurriedly put in order, the St. George's militia was called out, and a close watch for the enemy's squadron was kept from every point of vantage. On February 20 the storm broke, and soon Roseau was in a turmoil. Just before dawn on that day the alarm was fired from Scot's Head, or Kashakou (to give it its name in the local patois), that abrupt headland with jagged sandstone peaks, covered with wild scrub, forming the southern extremity of Soufrière Bay, which it protects from the winds and boisterous waves of the

164

Martinique Channel. From the fort at the end of this natural breakwater, formerly used as a quarantine and signal station, some strange armed vessels, flying the British colours, were seen making their way up to the Leeward coast. The news quickly spread to Roseau, drums beat to quarters, and the cobble-paved streets were soon thronged with troops, the local militia being strengthened by a small body of regulars who were speedily in readiness to receive the enemy.

The ships swept rapidly down to the town and the harbour-master boarded the foremost vessel. A blank cartridge was then fired from Fort Young, whereupon that official was taken prisoner; the British flag was then instantly lowered and that of France hoisted in its place, and there was no longer any doubt as to the nationality of the visitors. Ranging too near Fort Young, whose ramparts on a slight eminence in the town still bear the muzzle-loaders of a bygone age, they were met with a steady though ineffectual fire, which they were not slow in returning, but with as little effect.

Soon afterwards there came from under the lee a number of vessels which included the *Majestueux*, 120 guns, two seventy-fours, and several frigates and nineteen barges full of troops, which were rowed ashore under cover of the guns of two armed cruisers and seven other boats carrying carronades.

Preparations were promptly made to prevent General la Grange—for it was he who commanded the French troops—from effecting a landing near Roseau. Detachments of the West India Regiment and the militia

165

under Captain Serrant bore the brunt of the attack, assisted by the 46th Regiment of the line. The French, however, landed at Pointe Michel, two miles south of Roseau, marched northwards and met the defenders on the narrow pathway at Loubière over the pebbly beach at the foot of the high cliffs, which leads to Roseau.

Here our forces were supported by two field-pieces which, with a 24-pounder mounted on Melville's Battery, situated above the southern part of Roseau, now called "New Town" or "Charlotteville," did great execution. The French, with the cliff on their right and the waves lapping their feet on the left, were faced by a short piece of wall pierced for musketry, the venerable ruins of which, black with age and covered with bush and creepers, can still be seen close to the telegraph cable hut. For hour after hour they were held in check at this spot, but at about two o'clock in the afternoon, in spite of the stubborn resistance offered by General Prevost and his men, who contested every inch of the ground, the enemy, foiled at Loubière, succeeded under cover of the heavy guns of the French squadron in establishing their position at Woodbridge Bay. They then entered Roseau from the northern suburb and the defenders were withdrawn from Loubière. It was computed that at one time during the fighting more than 2000 of the enemy were opposed to only 200 British who, first under Major Mann, who was mortally wounded, and then under Captain O'Connell, kept their opponents, so greatly superior in numbers, at bay for over five hours, inflict-

A STREET IN ROSEAU, DOMINICA

ing a serious loss on them, after which the defenders effected an orderly retreat.

The ships tried in vain to silence the batteries, and it was only when the town was accidentally set on fire by the wads from the guns in Fort Young, deflected by the wind, that the spirited militia were compelled to fall back. With the permission of the Governor the Council then decided to surrender Roseau and its dependencies, stipulating that there should be no wanton pillage and that private property should be respected; but Roseau alone fell, and Prevost adhered to his determination to save the island.

The enemy encouraged by their success stormed Morne Daniel, the height which is now a part of Canefield Estate, about a mile to the north of Roseau and having carried the redoubt showed a disposition to cut the Governor off from the town and fort of Prince Rupert's. The enemy's ships were, moreover, pouring in an incessant fire from Woodbridge Bay (now better known as Goodwill Bay from the name of the adjacent sugar estate), and so, directing the regular troops to make forced marches across the island to Rosalie and to join him at Prince Rupert's, General Prevost made a dash for the fort there, which, accompanied by his staff, he succeeded in reaching in twenty-four hours with the aid of the Caribs. Here he was joined by the 46th Regiment and a light company of the 1st West India Regiment, which, under Capt. O'Connell, covered a most difficult tract of country by a series of brilliant forced marches in four days.

Having arrived at Prince Rupert's, Governor Prevost

hastily put the fort, which is situated in a hollow between two hills called the "Cabrits," forming the northern extremity of the bay, in a state of defence. Cattle were driven in and the tanks were filled with water from the North River. Lieut.-Colonel Broughton, who commanded the fort, having been apprised of the state of affairs by signal from Roseau, made judicious arrangements for the defence of the position. On February 25 a letter was received from la Grange summoning the garrison to surrender. The French general expressed his desire before beginning any military operations against the fort to fulfil a preliminary duty authorised and practised by civilised nations. Reminding the Governor of the melancholy fate of Roseau and the most cruel consequences which must attend the want of necessaries he urged him to accept the honourable conditions which he was prepared to grant, and thus to preserve the "interesting inhabitants" of the colony from fresh calamities. Prevost's reply was characteristic of the man who had commanded the troops during the Brigands' War in St. Vincent and had assisted in the recapture of St. Lucia in 1803. "My duty to my King and country," he said, "is so superior to every other consideration that I have only to thank you for the observations you have been pleased to make on the often inevitable consequences of war."

La Grange's attempt to intimidate the garrison into surrender was thus checkmated and, impressed by the formidable appearance of the fort, the French general re-embarked his force on the 27th and returned to

Roseau. Arrived there he demanded a ransom of
£20,000 currency, and threatened that if that sum
were not forthcoming within twenty-four hours he
would carry the members of the Legislature prisoners
to Guadeloupe. Eventually, however, he was satisfied
by the payment of £12,000, and after seizing all the
King's stores from the commissariat and every article
of value upon which he could lay his hands, as well as
a large number of negroes—who were subsequently
returned by Villaret Joyeuse, Governor of Martinique,
under a flag of truce—he withdrew his forces from
Dominica. For several days, however, he continued to
hover about off the island, and the *Vigilante*, tender to the
Centaur, Sir Samuel Hood's flagship, narrowly escaped
falling into his hands, being only saved by a heavy
covering fire from the guns of the fort. Finding that
the Dominicans with their seasoning of regulars were too
much for him General la Grange set sail with about
twenty of our merchantmen, which he found prepared
for sea, and was last seen off the south end of
Guadeloupe.

For his gallant defence of the island the House of
Assembly voted General Prevost a thousand guineas
with which to purchase a sword of honour and a service
of plate; from the Patriotic Fund he was granted
£100 for a sword and £200 for a piece of plate, and
he was also presented by the West India Committee
with a piece of plate to the value of three hundred
guineas in recognition of the "distinguished gallantry
and high military talents which he displayed." On his
return to England he was moreover rewarded with a

baronetcy; and, though his subsequent career in Canada during the war of 1812 was less successful, he will always be remembered as the man who saved Dominica.

Fort Young now serves as the barracks of the local police, and one of the guns which gave la Grange such a warm welcome is fired nightly at nine o'clock to tell the time to the peaceful inhabitants of Roseau and also on the arrival of the fortnightly mail steamer. On the wall of the Roseau Court House two tattered silken colours presented by Queen Charlotte to the St. George's Militia now rest. On their folds it is still possible to read the words " Woodbridge Bay " and " Pointe Michel."

The centenary of this memorable period was celebrated in Dominica in 1905, when an exchange of courtesies passed by cable between the officers of the Duke of Cornwall's Light Infantry—the old 46th— and Mr., now Sir H. Hesketh Bell, then Administrator of the island and now Governor of the Leeward Islands. A regimental dinner, at which a service of plate presented to the regiment a hundred years before by the grateful colonists was used, was also held in honour of the occasion.

CHAPTER VIII

ENGLISH HARBOUR, ANTIGUA

In the entire chain of West Indian islands there is no spot at once so romantic and so full of historic interest as English Harbour, which lies at the south-east corner of Antigua, the seat of government of the Leeward Islands.

This admirably sheltered haven, like so many others in the West Indies, is formed by the crater of a long extinct volcano; it is, in consequence, almost completely landlocked, being approached only by the narrowest of narrow entrances, barely a pistol-shot across. So secluded is the harbour indeed that, from the sea, it would need quite an experienced eye to detect the mouth, and one would imagine it to be just the sort of cove into which, in the old days, pirate vessels slipped to elude their pursuers.

English Harbour was, however, no resort for buccaneers and pirates, being well-known and highly valued by the commanders of his Majesty's ships of war as a safe anchorage from the earliest days of the colonisation of Antigua. Before propulsion by steam rendered seamen more independent of the weather, and enabled them, upon a warning fall in the barometer, to show a clean pair of heels before approaching cyclones,

171

it was much frequented in August, September and October, the dreaded hurricane months, and many vessels repaired to it to be careened and to refit.

On a promontory to the west of the entrance the crumbling remains of Fort Berkeley are still to be seen; on a spit of land to the east are those of the Horseshoe Battery. These defensive works and a chain boom rendered the harbour at one time secure from attack, while the sheltering hills to the north and east still protect it to a great extent from hurricanes. The phrase "to a great extent" is used advisedly, for no harbour, however well protected, could be deemed entirely free from the visitations of those terrible storms which occasionally ravage parts of the West Indies. It is indeed recorded in the *Antigua Herald and Gazette*, of August 28, 1848, that English Harbour did not escape the terrific hurricane of August 21-22 in that year, which caused such wide-spread destruction throughout the island.

The hills to the east, called after Governor Thomas Shirley, the Shirley Heights, once bristled with fortifications, while to the north the remains of Great George Fort, which covered no less than ten acres on Monks Hill, and was erected between the years 1689 and 1705 mainly as a place of refuge for the inhabitants in case of siege, bear testimony to the unique strength of the position.

On the west side the harbour is separated from the still larger Falmouth Harbour by a narrow isthmus called the Middle Ground, and it occurs at once to most visitors, as it did to an early governor of the

172

colony, what a magnificent harbour could be made by cutting a channel through this piece of land. In 1672 Sir Charles Wheeler, the governor in question, reporting on the state of the Leeward Islands, represented that "Antego has Falmouth Haven and the English Haven so contiguous that the neck of land between them may be cutt through and make a good harbr. against hurricanes. As the King of france has done at Martinico at 60,000 livres expence." Sir Charles Wheeler's advice was, however, not followed at that time, and it was not for many years after he had gone the way of all flesh that English Harbour was put in a state of defence.

It was left to two naval officers, Captain Francis Cooper, of H.M.S. *Lynn*, and Captain Del Garno, of H.M.S. *South Sea Castle*, to share the credit for calling attention to the great advantages which would accrue from providing a suitable place in the West Indies for careening and refitting vessels, and from thus obviating the need of sending ships all the way to the North American colonies for the purpose; they it was who early in the eighteenth century warmly advocated the establishment of a dockyard at English Harbour. Their suggestions were adopted, and work on the first part of the dockyard—that known as St. Helena—was begun in 1726, two plots of land, each ten acres in extent, being granted to the King for the purpose by an Act passed by the Legislature on September 25 in the preceding year. This land had been given to Joseph Green and William Greatrix, privates in H.M. forces, which had been disbanded on the close of the war, but was forfeited to the local government consequent upon the failure of the two soldiers to develop it.

The work of designing the yard was entrusted to Captain Del Garno. He was instructed to erect "wharves, magazines and storehouses . . . for the use of men-of-war of the Leeward Islands squadron." The Legislature built the wharf and the fort at the entrance to the harbour, while the King defrayed the cost of the storehouses, &c., "besides supplying cannons and warlike stores." The Legislature also made a further contribution to the defences of the island by passing an Act, on February 8, 1733, providing for the construction of two brick cisterns forty feet long by ten feet wide and ten feet deep—a very necessary precaution in an island where fresh water is scarce—as well as a platform of one hundred feet square for furnishing a good supply of water to his Majesty's ships. The captain was awarded two hundred guineas "for his services in constructing the wharf and platform at English Harbour" on January 5, 1727-8. Captain Del Garno was also responsible for carrying out the more elaborate works on the opposite side of the harbour which were completed in 1743. For this extension of the yard a piece of land was purchased from one Thomas Bodkin, five acres being appropriated for the dockyard and the remainder allotted to poor white settlers at the discretion of the Governor and the Legislature.

Some idea of the appearance of the harbour towards the end of the eighteenth century is conveyed by a

ENGLISH HARBOUR, ANTIGUA

The building among the trees on the left is Clarence House

report contained in a letter from Governor Sir Thomas Shirley, dated November 3, 1781.

"English Harbour lies," he wrote, "to the southward . . . and is surrounded on every side with lofty hills, which defend it from the winds. On account of the depth and perpetual smoothness of the water, the narrowness of its entrance, and some other advantages, it is the best harbour in any of the British West India Islands if we except Jamaica. On the West side of the entrance of this harbour is a small redoubt, known by the name of Fort Barclay. It stands in a commanding situation, and is well calculated to annoy an enemy, should an attack on that quater be attempted. The opposite rising ground at the mouth of this harbour also contains a stone defence, which commands an extensive view of the sea. There are besides many little batteries in various parts of the vicinity which are judiciously placed, and if well defended would oblige an enemy of superior numbers and strength, either to relinquish an attack upon the dock yard, or to pay with considerable loss for the advantage of taking or destroying it."

Viewed from the hills above, the aspect of the harbour is picturesque in the extreme. On a stone jetty with irregular but sharply defined edges across the water is a group of yellow buildings with red roofs in pleasing contrast to the deep blue of the water, which as often as not is unbroken by even a ripple. These are the naval barracks, capstan house, storehouses and repairing sheds and the usual dockyard buildings, which once resounded with the roar of the forges and the cries of the artificers. Below is the oldest part of the dockyard, that known as St. Helena, alongside which, down to the middle of last century, the largest ships afloat could be berthed. To the south of this is the secluded anchorage called Freeman's Bay.

The harbour used to have a terrible and only too well-deserved reputation for unhealthiness. The dreaded " Yellow Jack " and malaria played havoc with the crews, who were crowded into stuffy barracks, while their vessels were being careened alongside the wharves. During the rainy season, which coincided with the hurricane months, when the harbour was full of shipping, existence there must have been well-nigh intolerable. Mosquitoes abounded, and it is not to be wondered at that the place was considered a perfect hot-bed of fever and disease.

Captain Edward Thomson in one of his " Sailor's Letters" draws a graphic picture of its discomforts. On October 21, 1756, he wrote : " With the strictest truth I may call this one of the most infernal places on the face of the globe, though a commodious harbour for refitting. I have long been suffering from a white flux, and for recovery am stuffed into a small room with twenty-six people. I officiate as chaplain, and bury eight a morning. I attribute the fever to water taken from cisterns built by Admiral Knowles. It is all rain-water, and covered close up, which for want of air breeds poisonous animalculæ and becomes foul and putrid."

176

It is tantalizing to think how very near Captain Thomson was to discovering the real communicating agent of infection in yellow fever—the dreaded little *stegomyia* mosquito. Thomson believed that fevers were caused by water which, becoming foul, bred poisonous animalculæ. What a little way it seems to the discovery that it was the mosquito bred on stagnant water, and not the water *per se*, which was really to be feared; and yet it was not until nearly a hundred and forty years after this time that Doctor Manson and Professor Ross proved that it was the *anopheles* mosquito which was the source of infection in the case of malaria, and six years later that Finlay enunciated the theory that the *stegomyia* performed a similar function in yellow fever—a theory the correctness of which was proved by those heroes Reed, Carroll, Agramonte and Lazear.

The mortality from yellow fever at the period with which we are dealing was literally appalling. It was by no means uncommon for whole crews to be stricken down by the fell disease. In May 1793, for example, his Majesty's ship *Experiment* arrived off English Harbour in a state of great distress, having lost nearly all her men from fever. To such straits, indeed, was she reduced that it became necessary to send a boat's crew from the *Solebay* to warp her into the harbour. Every man of that crew died and the contagion was communicated to their own ship, of whose company no fewer than two hundred men perished.

An artificer from the Ordnance, who slept on board, caught the fever, and the infection was carried—

by a blanket and wearing apparel it was then believed, though we now know that that could not be the case—to a whole detachment of artillery, and to the 31st Regiment which was then on garrison duty.

It quickens the pulse to feel that the weather-beaten walls of these dockyard buildings have witnessed the comings and going of so many of our distinguished naval commanders of the brilliant eighteenth century, of Benbow, Rodney, Hood, Jervis, and of the greatest of all, Nelson himself.

With the memory of the hero of Trafalgar the harbour must for ever be closely associated, and if it were only for Nelson's connection with it the old buildings and wharves would surely be deserving of preservation as a national monument by the people of the West Indies.

Nelson was appointed to the *Boreas*, 28 guns, in March 1784, the year following that in which the American War was brought to a close, and he sailed in her in the following May for the Leeward Islands.

This was not his first visit to the West Indies. Already, in 1771, as a boy of thirteen, he had made a voyage to those colonies and back in a merchant ship belonging to Messrs. Hibbert, Purrier and Horton. He had served, too, in various of his Majesty's ships on the Jamaica station between 1777 and 1782, a period of great anxiety in the colony, which was in constant fear of invasion by the French—a fear which was only removed by Rodney's memorable victory over de Grasse in the Battle of the Saints off Dominica on April 12, 1782. It was during this period that

178

Nelson was for a time entrusted with the command of the batteries of Fort Charles at Port Royal, where the wooden " quarter-deck," along which he used to pace, is still pointed out to visitors. On the crumbling walls of this picturesque old fort, now bright with many beautiful tropical flowers, among which the exquisite pink corallita creeper predominates, a tablet bears the stirring inscription:

IN THIS PLACE

DWELT

HORATIO NELSON

YOU WHO TREAD IN HIS FOOTPRINTS

REMEMBER HIS GLORY.

On reaching English Harbour in 1784 Nelson found that he was senior captain, and therefore second in command. This being the case he declined to take orders from Captain Moutray, the Commissioner of the dockyard, who had hoisted a commodore's broad pennant in H.M.S. *Latona*, then moored to one of the wharves. Nelson claimed that though the Commissioner was twenty-one years his senior in rank, that officer was only on half-pay and was not, therefore, entitled to hoist a broad pennant, and he accordingly gave orders for it to be struck. To show, however, that he bore the Commissioner no ill-will personally, he dined with him that same night and Moutray and his wife were thereafter among Nelson's few valued friends on the Leeward Islands' station. Nelson frequently visited their residence at Windsor. In a letter to Mr. William

Locker, dated September 24, 1784, he wrote : "Was it not for Mrs. Moutray, who is *very very* good to me, I should almost hang myself at this infernal hole."

The merchants were at this time engaged in a contraband trade with the Americans, in contravention of the Navigation Act which forbade intercourse with the United States, and it was to the bad feeling engendered by his determination to enforce that Act that Nelson's dislike of the Leeward Islands was, no doubt, largely due. "English Harbour I hate the sight of," he wrote in one of his letters. In another he referred to it as a "vile hole," while from St. Kitts he wrote "Every day convinces (me) how superior the Jamaica station is to this."

It must be remembered that the sympathies of the inhabitants were largely with the revolted colonists and that, except in the Bahamas, which became a haven for many of the United Empire Loyalists, the loyalists were in a decided minority. On St. Patrick's day, the Irish colours, bearing thirteen stripes, were freely displayed, a circumstance which so incensed Nelson that he excused himself from keeping an engagement to dine with the President of St. Kitts as a protest against his permitting such a state of affairs to exist. General Thomas Shirley, who had shared with General Fraser the honours of the defence of Brimstone Hill in St. Kitts, in the early months of 1782, and was still Governor of the Leeward Islands, declined to suppress the illegal trade with America, saying that "old generals were not in the habit of taking advice from young gentlemen," a taunt to which the young captain replied : "I am as old as the Prime Minister of England, and think myself as capable of commanding one of his Majesty's ships as that Minister is of governing the State."

The Americans, taking advantage of the registers of their ships, which were issued to them before the Declaration of Independence in 1782 while they were still in the eye of the law British subjects, were conducting an illegal but very lucrative trade with the islands. Nelson, who showed much moral courage, despite the opposition of the Governor, the Customs' officers, the people, and even of Admiral Sir Richard Hughes himself, determined that the Navigation Act should be rigidly enforced.

The crisis arose when the young captain found four American vessels deeply laden with merchandise flying the island colours off Nevis. He at once ordered the captains to hoist their own flag, and on their refusing to do so sent for some of their crew and examined them in his cabin. The men admitted that the ships were American and forthwith the vessels were seized.

The greatest indignation thereupon prevailed. Subscriptions were hastily raised and Nelson was prosecuted in the colonial courts, damages amounting to £40,000 being claimed. For eight weeks Nelson remained aboard the *Boreas* to escape arrest, and it was not until he had been promised the protection of the judge that he went ashore for the day. Even then an attempt was made to arrest him, an attempt which was only frustrated by the intervention of Mr. Herbert, the President of Nevis. Nelson at the trial successfully pleaded his cause and the vessels were condemned. While these matters were proceeding, he sent home a lengthy memorial to the King. As the result of this, orders were issued for his defence at the expense of the Crown, and as the outcome of his suggestions the Register Act was passed, which eventually put an end to the illicit traffic. It was in connection with his treatment at Nevis that Nelson foretold that one day he would have a Gazette all to himself.

While on the Leeward Islands station, Nelson became afflicted with what, in the case of a daughter of Sir Richard Hughes, he called " the disorder which is what the world calls love," and it was not long after meeting Frances Herbert Nisbet, the charming niece of Mr. Herbert, the President of the Council of Nevis, that he became engaged to her, and among his letters are many addressed from English Harbour to his " Dearest Fanny," from which the following are characteristic extracts: ". . . I have not been able to get even a cottage upon a hill, notwithstanding my utmost endeavours; and therefore have been kept here, most woefully pinched by mosquitoes, for my sins, perhaps ; so the generous inhabitants of Antigua think, I suppose ; not one of whom has been here, or has asked me to leave English Harbour.

" . . . As you begin to know something about sailors, have you not often heard, that salt water and absence always wash away love ? Now, I am such a heretic as not to believe that faith; for behold, every morning since my arrival, I have had six pails of salt water at

182

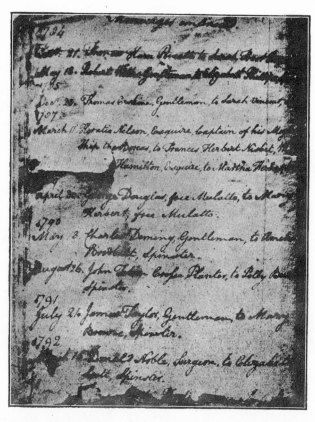

THE RECORD OF NELSON'S MARRIAGE TO FRANCES NISBET
IN THE REGISTER AT FIG-TREE CHURCH, NEVIS

daylight poured upon my head, and instead of finding what the seamen say to be true, I perceive the contrary effect; and if it goes on so contrary to the prescription, you must see me before my fixed time. At first, I bore absence tolerably, but now it is almost insupportable; and by-and-by I expect it will be quite so. But patience is a virtue, and I must exercise it upon this occasion, whatever it costs my feelings. . . . The moment old *Boreas* is habitable in my cabin, I shall fly to it, to avoid mosquitoes and melancholies. Hundreds of the former are now devouring me through all my clothes. You will, however, find I am better; though when you see me, I shall be like an Egyptian mummy, for the heat is intolerable. But I walk a mile out at night without fatigue, and all day I am housed. A quart of goats' milk is also taken every day, and I enjoy English sleep, always barring mosquitoes, which all Frank's care with my net cannot keep out at present."

The marriage was eventually celebrated on March 11, 1787, at Montpelier House in Nevis.

Alas! of the original Montpelier House only the ruined walls and the gate posts now remain; but a granite tablet placed on one of the latter by permission of the present owner, Mr. J. H. Sampson, records the connection of the place with the hero of Trafalgar. It is inscribed:

ON THIS SITE STOOD
MONTPELIER HOUSE
WHEREIN
ON THE 11TH DAY OF MARCH 1787

WEST INDIAN TALES

HORATIO NELSON
OF IMMORTAL MEMORY
THEN CAPTAIN OF THE BOREAS
WAS MARRIED TO
FRANCES HERBERT NISBET.

Mrs. Nisbet, then in her eighteenth year, was the widow of Dr. Nisbet, a physician, and she had one little boy named Josiah. Prince William Henry, an old shipmate of Nelson's, who had arrived at English Harbour in the preceding winter, insisted on giving the bride away.

Prince William Henry, who afterwards became Duke of Clarence and King William IV., had already been in the West Indies in 1782, under Viscount Hood, and had met Nelson while on the Jamaica station. He was appointed to the command of the *Pegasus*, 28 guns, in 1786 when he was just of age, and he sailed in her to Antigua, where he remained for upwards of a year. During this period he continued on the terms of the closest intimacy with Nelson, who accompanied him wherever he went.

We are told by John Luffman* that the arrival of the Prince put the small community into a ferment. Addresses were presented to him by the Legislature and by the merchants, expressive of loyalty to his Royal father and of the happiness and honour conferred on them by his gracious visit. The Address of the

* A brief account of the Island of Antigua in letters to a friend written in the years 1786, 1787, 1788, by John Luffman.

Legislature was presented by Mr. John Burke, Solicitor-General of the Leeward Islands, who unfortunately broke down completely under the strain of addressing royalty. "Notwithstanding this gentleman has been for years hackneyed at the bar," wrote Luffman, "and is a bold orator, yet, on this occasion, to the astonishment of every bystander, he was nearly bereft of the power of utterance."

The Prince was entertained at dinners, cock-fights, and balls, and a round of amusements was prepared for his benefit. "The Prince opened both balls, with a Miss A——, a beautiful young lady of respectable family, and his affability, politeness, and condescension, to every person who had the honor of his conversation, was as conspicuous as it was pleasing. The ladies put their best smiles on their faces and their best adornments on their persons; indeed, every individual seemed emulous of showing respect to the Royal visitor. Many offers of particular attention and civility have been made to his Highness, which he, in general, declined, wishing rather to appear in the humble character of a private gentleman than in the dignified situation of a Prince. How long he means to honor this isle with his presence, I cannot with certainty learn, it will probably be several months; the people here, I believe, hope and wish it may be for years."

The islands vied with one another in complimenting the Prince and lavishing gifts upon him. During one of his cruises the House of Assembly of Barbados presented him with a gold-hilted sword valued at three hundred guineas, while the Council and Assembly of

185

Dominica offered for his acceptance a "time-piece" of equal value. The House of Assembly of Jamaica, not to be outdone, waited upon him in a body at Port Royal when he revisited the island in the *Andromeda* in 1788 to tender their congratulations, and on December 2 they voted him a thousand guineas to be laid out in the purchase of an elegant star, ornamented with diamonds, to be presented to him, as "an humble testimony of the very high respect and esteem the island entertained for his eminent virtues, and the happiness they felt in seeing him among them; as well as the grateful sense they had of the particular attention paid by his Royal Highness to the duties of a profession which was the support and defence of the British Empire in general and of that island in particular." At a later date the same body voted three thousand guineas to purchase a piece of plate, to be presented to him as "a testimony of their sense of his great parliamentary services in the important question relative to the African slave-trade."

To the negroes the Prince was the "Grand Buccra." His presence among them caused them the liveliest satisfaction, and he was invariably mobbed when he took his walks abroad. The *Gentleman's Magazine* for 1787 gives us a few particulars regarding the demeanour of his Royal Highness at this time. He was, it states, "quite the gentleman and so keen on his profession that until he arrived at English Harbour, when the *Pegasus* was careened, and he was bound to go ashore, he never slept off the ship; further, he attended to every little detail, delivering his own orders with the most minute attention to the duty and the discipline of his ship." Indeed, the Prince was such a strict disciplinarian that it was said that no officer could serve under him "but that sooner or later he must be broke." On one occasion, for example, he had a violent quarrel with his first lieutenant, Isaac Schomberg, who was an officer of experience, twelve years his senior, which resulted in Nelson sending the *Pegasus* to Jamaica, where the Commodore, Admiral Gardner, succeeded in smoothing matters over by appointing Schomberg to another vessel.

For the benefit of his Royal Highness a substantial residence was erected on a plateau on the hill facing the dockyard at English Harbour, stonemasons being brought out from England for the express purpose of its construction. The house, which was afterwards called Clarence House, stands there yet. Until the dockyard was abandoned it was used as the admiral's residence, and no doubt filled a long-felt want; for in Nelson's day Admiral Sir Richard Hughes, in the absence of any official residence, lived in a boarding-house in Barbados! Clarence House is now the country-seat—and a very charming one at that—of the Governor of the Leeward Islands.

During the hurricane season—between August and October—English Harbour was invariably full of shipping, and Nelson encouraged all sorts of amusements to keep his men happy and fit, such as music, dancing and cudgelling, a pastime which was very much in vogue in the West Indies in those days, as some old engravings show. Again, he never allowed the ships under his command to remain long at any particular island, and the result of these precautions was that not a single man in the *Boreas* died during the three years she was on the station, although the Leeward Islands was considered a notoriously unhealthy one.

The officers, too, would get up amateur theatricals to pass the time during the rainy season. Luffman, in one of his letters writes: "Our theatre has attractions, whether it is owing to the abilities of the gentlemen performers, or from the attentions paid the fair, who visit it in great numbers, is not for me to determine, but we have generally good houses." Again: "Our theatricals go on well, since I last wrote to you on that head, several pieces have been brought out, and received with an applause that cannot fail to be gratifying to the gentlemen concerned in these amusements. The 'Orphan,' 'King Henry the Fourth,' 'West Indian,' 'Lethe,' and 'Lying Valet,' are among those already played, and 'King Lear.' 'The Fair Penitent,' 'Jane Shore,' and several farces are getting in readiness. . . . I was at the play on the 10th, 'Jane Shore,' and for want of females in the dramatic walk, our representative of the lovely Jane, ' once the fairest amongst English dames,' was a *gentleman* . . . the parts of Hastings and Dumant were well filled; indeed, Mr. M—t—n, the gentleman who performed the latter character, is a finished actor. Notwithstanding the aid of ventilators, and although a part of the roofing boards were removed also for the more free admission of air, I suffered much from the extreme heat of the house; a most violent headache was the consequence, from which I am now hardly recovered."

A VIEW OF ENGLISH HARBOUR, ANTIGUA, IN THE YEAR 1800

After the drawing by Mr. Pocock from a sketch by Captain Walter Tremenheere

For the officers a regular mess was established, which no doubt added to the amenities of life in the harbour. One of Nelson's letters dated English Harbour, August 3, 1784, runs : " As the captains of the navy at this port mean to establish a mess for the hurricane months, by their desire I write to beg that you will send us round, by the first opportunity, the undermentioned articles, viz : one hogshead of port, one of the best white wine that you have, twelve dozen of porter in bottles, fifty pounds of loaf sugar, one firkin of good butter, two baskets of salt, two pounds black pepper.

" P.S.—As we only wait for these things to begin our mess, the sooner they arrive the better. Mr. Druce, the agent victualler is a going to send provisions round for the *Fury* which will be a good opportunity."

That there was a good deal of hard drinking on the station in those days may be taken for granted, but Nelson did not err in this respect. In a letter which Mrs. Nisbet received from a friend before her second marriage, the following was said of the captain of the *Boreas:* " We have at last seen the Captain of the *Boreas*, of whom so much has been said. He came up just before dinner, much heated, and was very silent ; yet seemed, according to the old adage, to think the more. He declined drinking any wine; but after dinner, when the President, as usual, gave the following toasts, ' the King,' ' the Queen and Royal Family,' and ' Lord Hood,' this strange man regularly filled his glass, and observed, that those were always bumper toasts with him ; which having drank, he uniformly passed

189

the bottle, and relapsed into his former taciturnity. It was impossible, during this visit, for any of us to make out his real character ; there was such a reserve and sternness in his behaviour, with occasional sallies, though very transient, of a superior mind. Being placed by him, I endeavoured to rouse his attention by showing him all the civilities in my power ; but I drew out little more than ' Yes ' and ' No.' "

Nelson revisited Antigua in 1805 during his famous pursuit of Villeneuve to the West Indies and back before Trafalgar, and it is a tradition that he refitted his ships at English Harbour on that occasion. No doubt many of his ships availed themselves of the dockyard, but it is certain Nelson himself did not go ashore.

The whole of Villeneuve's fleet lay off St. John's on June 8, and a landing was hourly expected. Lord Lavington, the Governor—whose remains now lie in a crude tomb under a sapodilla tree on Carlisle's estate— hastily mustered 500 men to defend the island. To the great relief of the inhabitants, however, the French ships sailed on June 13, and a few hours after their departure, Lord Nelson, who had been in close pursuit, anchored off St. John's with twelve battleships of the line. He could not, however, be persuaded to land, and wrote to Lord Lavington from on board H.M.S. *Victory*, expressing his determination not to lose one moment in pushing after the enemy, " and his persuasion that they were gone to Cadiz and Toulon, flattering themselves with the hopes of getting Egypt."

A few years after Nelson's sojourn at English Harbour, a tragedy occurred there which was for many years the talk of every branch of his Majesty's service. The chief actors in the affair were Thomas Pitt, second Baron Camelford, and Lieutenant Charles Peterson, both of his Majesty's navy.

On the brick-paved wharf, under the shadow of the now deserted barracks and dockyard buildings, lies a large anchor, resting on a cement pedestal. It bears no inscription, but many say it was placed there to mark the spot where this tragedy took place. Others, however, will tell you—and they will probably be right— that it is merely one of the several anchors used in the old days for careening his Majesty's ships of war. Be that as it may, it is certain that the deplorable episode which will now be related took place near where it stands.

Pitt, a cousin of William Pitt, was born in 1775, and after passing his early years in Switzerland, and receiving his education at the Charterhouse, entered the navy in 1789, and succeeded his father, the first Lord Camelford, four years later. High-spirited, and reckless to a degree, he was constantly getting into trouble, and he had already been marooned at Hawaii for insubordination, had served before the mast, and had been summarily discharged from the *Resistance*—of which he was appointed acting lieutenant—before he succeeded through influence in securing the appointment of lieutenant commander of H.M. sloop of war *Favourite*, on the Leeward Islands station in 1797.

Camelford, although only two and twenty years of age, had already earned no mean reputation as a

191

duellist, and his quick temper involved him in many disputes.

Instances of the total lack of self-restraint which he showed when his anger was aroused are numerous. As an example, an episode which occurred in Grenada in 1797 may be cited. Two hours after sunset on October 25 in that year a suspicious vessel, showing no lights, was seen approaching the little town of Gouyave, whereupon a detachment of the 2nd West India Regiment, which was stationed there under the command of Captain McDonald, fired a gun at her from the battery. The mysterious vessel at once responded by directing several broadsides at the fort and town.

The battery returned the compliment as fast as its single gun could be loaded, and the suspicious vessel eventually sheered off, but not before most of the inhabitants had fled in a state of panic towards St. George's, in the belief that the French were endeavouring to effect a landing. In that town the sound of the firing was heard distinctly, and all possible precautions were taken against attack, which was momentarily expected.

At daybreak next morning, H.M.S. *Favourite* was seen lying quiety at anchor in St. George's Harbour, and it was ascertained that it was her commander, Captain Lord Camelford, who was responsible for the bombardment of a peaceable town. It never occurred to him that his stealthy movements might be capable of misinterpretation ; and considering himself insulted by the firing of the solitary gun in the fort, he retaliated in the vigorous manner described above. The Governor,

AN OLD FORT AT ENGLISH HARBOUR, ANTIGUA

CAMELFORD'S ANCHOR, ENGLISH HARBOUR, ANTIGUA

Colonel Charles Green, was justly indignant ; and, to make matters worse, Lord Camelford, who called upon him, treated his Excellency in a most disrespectful manner.

Peterson, the first lieutenant of the *Favourite*, very naturally resented Camelford, who was two years his junior, being put over his head. He accordingly applied for and succeeded in obtaining promotion to the *Perdrix*, then commanded by Captain William C. Fahie (a native, by the way, of St. Kitts) who had distinguished himself by his plucky attempt to communicate with the garrison during the siege of Brimstone Hill in 1782.

Towards the end of 1797 the *Favourite* and the *Perdrix* were ordered to English Harbour to refit and remained there about two months. Camelford and Peterson were, in consequence, necessarily thrown very much together ; and, if we are to believe Captain Henry Mitford of his Majesty's ship *Matilda*, there was " a good deal of bad blood existing between the two parties." Such at any rate was the " dispassionate opinion " which he expressed, in a report to Admiral Harvey, then Commander-in-Chief of the Leeward Islands station.

There was, however, no actual rupture between the two officers until one fateful day—it was the 13th— in the following January, when Fahie happened to be absent on leave, and Peterson as his representative and as senior officer to Camelford on the lieutenants' list claimed to be senior officer on the station. Then the long-standing feud between the two officers was brought to a head.

It was the custom in those troublous days for boats to patrol the harbour throughout the night, the various vessels there taking it in turn to furnish the necessary crews for the purpose, and Camelford, as commander of the *Favourite*, refusing to recognise Peterson's claim to superior rank, sent a peremptory order to him to " row guard," as it was called. This Peterson refused point-blank to do and shortly afterwards that officer despatched a counter-order to Camelford.

In a furious rage Camelford thereupon sent a message to Lieutenant Clement Milward, instructing him to cross the harbour at once with a squad of marines, to arrest Peterson, and to bring him to the easternmost capstan house dead or alive. A mistake was made in the delivery of the message by Lieutenant Parsons and there was some procrastination, which enabled Peterson to make preparations for resistance, and when Milward reached the mess-room where that officer was, he was confronted by two sentries whom Peterson had instructed to guard the staircase. After a short parley Milward was allowed to ascend; but when Peterson seized a brace of pistols he discreetly withdrew, and recrossing the harbour reported the progress of events to Camelford.

Peterson now descended the stairs, calling out: " *Perdrix's, Perdrix's,* arm yourselves," and the armourer, acting on his instructions, served out muskets, bayonets, cartouche-boxes and cutlasses to the bewildered men.

Meanwhile Camelford, hearing the noise, crossed the

harbour with all the marines he could muster, and paraded them in front of the sailors of the *Perdrix*, who were ordered by their misguided commander to load with ball cartridge and to fix bayonets.

Camelford now called out: "Where is Lieutenant Peterson?"

"Here I am, sir, damme," replied that officer.

"Do you still persist in disobeying my command?" shouted Camelford.

"I do," replied Peterson.

Camelford, seizing a pistol from Lieutenant Milward, repeated his question a second time, and failing to get a satisfactory reply then presented the weapon at Peterson and shot him, the unfortunate officer falling mortally wounded in a pool of blood near the spot where the anchor already referred to now stands.

For a moment there was a dead silence, and Camelford, fully expecting that the men of the *Perdrix* would avenge the death of their commander, shouted out that he had shot Peterson for mutiny, and called upon Crawford to dismiss the men.

Crawford then, to quote his own statement, gave the order: "Stop, avast loading your pieces, Mr. Peterson is shot! Return your arms! Dismiss!"

Fortunately the men at once obeyed the instructions, and all fear of mutiny was at an end and further bloodshed averted.

At the inquest which was held on the following day in one of the dockyard buildings before Richard Bowman, coroner, the jury, of which William Hill was foreman, found that Peterson met his death as a result of mutiny, but they were unable to say whether it was Camelford or Peterson who was guilty of that offence. Camelford, anxious to have the matter cleared up, now applied for a court-martial. His request was conceded by Admiral Harvey, and the Court assembled on board his Majesty's ship the *Invincible* in Fort Royal Bay, Martinique, on January 20.

Captain Cayley of the flagship was President of the Court, the other members of which were Captains Jemmet Mainwaring, Richard Browne, Charles Elkins, and Alex. S. Burrowes. The proceedings lasted four days, during which a mass of evidence was taken, and on January 25 Camelford was acquitted and handed back his sword. It was found on the other hand that it was Peterson who had been guilty of mutiny, the judgment of the court being couched in the following terms : "The very extraordinary and manifest disobedience of Lieutenant Peterson, both before and at the instant of his death, to the lawful orders of Lord Camelford, the senior officer at English Harbour at that time, and the violent measures taken by Lieutenant Peterson to resist the same, by arming the *Perdrix's* ship's company, were acts of mutiny highly injurious to the discipline of His Majesty's service—the Court do therefore unanimously adjudge that the Right Honourable Lord Camelford be honourably acquitted." *

* Minutes of the Proceedings of a Court-Martial, assembled and held on board His Majesty's ship the *Invincible*, in Fort Royal Bay, Martinique, on the 20th of January, 1798, and continued by Adjournment (Sunday excepted) until the 25th to try ―― for the death of ―― London MDCCXCIX.

In spite of the finding, many people still maintained that Peterson was really the senior officer, and it was believed in some quarters that the court was influenced by the dread of "mutiny," for it must be remembered that the Mutiny of the Nore which created such a sensation had taken place less than a year before and was still being discussed wherever sailors foregathered.

Though Camelford was afterwards promoted, his subsequent career, which was the reverse of creditable, tended to increase the sympathy which was felt with the young officer whose promising career he had so abruptly brought to a close. Being suspected of having communicated with the French, Camelford was superseded in the command of the *Charon*, and in a fit of temper this hot-headed peer then removed his name from the books of the navy.

The closing years of his life were spent in London, where his escapades became the talk of the town. Many were the stories told about him; how he offered to go to Paris and kidnap Napoleon and bring him to England, and how he threatened to put his negro servant into the House of Commons for a Pocket Borough. On one occasion we find him being fined £500 for throwing a Mr. Humphries down the stairs of a theatre ; on another we hear of him wildly laying about him with a club in the midst of a mob which had gathered outside his lodgings in Bond Street to protest against his failure to illuminate them at the Peace of 1801. Then the story is told of how two eye-witnesses of one of his quarrels, on calling with an offer to give evidence to the effect that he had been assaulted, precipitately left on seeing over one of the mantelpieces a thick bludgeon and a perfect pyramid of offensive weapons surmounted by a horsewhip.

Camelford in 1804 met more than his match at last. Hearing that Captain Best had spoken slightingly of him, he challenged that officer to a duel. Captain Best was a "Barbadian born," to use the familiar West Indian expression. He owned two estates in Barbados—"Moonshine," now the property of Mr. F. C. Bancroft, in the parish of St. George, and "Fairy Valley" in Christ Church, which now belongs to the Messrs. Yearwood. No doubt Camelford met Best when he was on the Leeward Islands station, and the two were boon companions until the quarrel arose. Every effort was made by friends of the parties to effect a reconciliation, but the high-spirited nobleman was obdurate, believing that if he refused to fight his reputation would suffer, as Best was considered the finest shot in England.

The encounter accordingly took place on March 7, 1804. To avoid the possibility of arrest Camelford left his lodgings between 1 and 2 A.M. on the previous morning and passed the night in a tavern. Soon after daybreak on the 7th he met his antagonist in a field to the west of Holland House, Kensington, near what is now the Melbury Road. Struck by Best's first shot, he fell mortally wounded. He was carried to Little Holland House, where he was attended by a surgeon named Knight, who at once pronounced the case hopeless.

198

Camelford, after lingering a few days, died on March 10, in the presence of his most intimate friend, Captain Barry, at the early age of 29.

The inquest was held at the White Hart, near by, and, after hearing the evidence of Lord Holland's servants and the report of the surgeon, the jury returned a verdict of "wilful murder against some person or persons unknown."

There the matter ended, and Best was never brought to trial; for Camelford, in his will which he had drawn up just before the duel, had made it clear that he himself was the aggressor. "There are many matters," he wrote, "which, at another time, I might be inclined to mention; but I will say nothing more at present than that, in the present contest, I am fully and entirely the aggressor, as well in the spirit as the letter of the word; should I therefore lose my life in a contest of my own seeking, I most solemnly forbid any of my friends or relations, let them be of whatsoever description they may, from instituting any vexatious proceedings against my antagonist; and should, notwithstanding the above declaration on my part, the law of the land be put in force against him, I desire that this part of my will may be made known to the King, in order that his royal heart may be moved to extend his mercy towards him." *

The body was moved to Camelford House, Park Lane; and, after temporarily resting in St. Ann's,

* "The Annual Register," 1804, p. 472.

Soho, where it was laid on March 17, it was buried in Switzerland in accordance with instructions left in a codicil to the will. In this remarkable document, Camelford gave minute particulars as to where he wanted to be buried, prefacing the expression of his wish to lie in Switzerland by stating that persons in general have a strong attachment to the country which gave them birth, and on their death-bed usually desire their remains to be conveyed to their native land, however distant it may be. "I wish my body to be removed as soon as may be convenient to a country far distant! to a spot not near the haunts of men; but where the surrounding scenery may smile upon my remains . . . Let no monument or stone be placed over my grave."

After the duel Best went abroad "for the benefit of his health." For some years he resided in seclusion, and then settled at Long's Hotel in Bond Street, where he lived apart from his wife, who was Lady Emily Stratford. He had one son, John Stratford Best, and a daughter, Elizabeth, who became Lady Tollemache; but the family is now believed to be extinct.

The subsequent history of the old dockyard in Antigua has been comparatively uneventful, except for the punishing which it received from the hurricane on August 21 and 22, 1848, which struck it with full force. Recording that event the *Antigua Herald and Gazette* stated: "At English Harbour the violence of the storm was fully felt, very few buildings indeed escaped the most serious injury.

ENGLISH HARBOUR, ANTIGUA

There are not many houses left in a habitable state. At the dockyard the officers' quarters —a fine pile of substantial buildings known as ‘Albion Row’—have been levelled with the earth, and the capstan house has been destroyed. At the Ridge the soldiers' barracks have been reduced to a heap of ruins. We have been informed that Colonel Fane had a narrow escape—that officer's quarters having been blown down soon after he had left them for a place of greater security. At Dow's Hill, the Governor's country seat—the north portion of the dwelling house was blown in and a considerable quantity of furniture much damaged. The stables were much damaged, in the fall of a part of which two horses were killed and another seriously bruised. At Middle Ground the barracks were totally destroyed. The troops are all quartered in tents. The only buildings on the Ridge that escaped are the Artillery barracks, the Commissary's residence and the hospital."

When there was no longer any need of opportunities for careening vessels, the old sailing ships being replaced by steam and steel, the glory of English Harbour began to wane. For many years the old harbour was better known as the port of call of the intercolonial mail steamer—as which it was used until St. John's took its place—than as a naval dockyard; but it was not until 1889 that it was finally abandoned by the Admiralty. Even now it is occasionally entered by ships of war during their cruises in West Indian waters. Our present King George V. has visited it on more than one occasion in H.M.S. *Canada*, and an inscription written by him on the wall of one of the barracks, "A Merry Xmas and Happy New Year 2 You All," is still pointed out.

It is to be feared that the dockyard buildings are now rapidly falling into decay in spite of the loving care of the Hon. Arthur W. Holmes à Court, a former Director of Public Works of Antigua, who is privileged to reside in the Harbour Master's residence among them. With its unique associations the harbour should be preserved as an historic site. To the British visitor it must always have a deep interest and fascination; and it is to be hoped that the far-seeing Legislature of the island may some day provide adequate funds to save English Harbour from further damage and destruction.

CHAPTER IX

OLD CARTAGENA

MOST mail steamers on their voyage between Trinidad and Colon call at one or more ports on the Spanish Main, the historic littoral of Colombia and Venezuela so rich in memories of the days of Spain's greatness, and of Drake and the buccaneers who infested the Caribbean and preyed on her treasure ships. Of these ports on the Tierra Firma of the spacious days, Cartagena is the most notable, not only because of its size and comparative importance, but also on account of the wealth of romance which surrounds it.

Those who wish to see Colon as well as Cartagena should visit the last-named place on their way from and not to Colon, for the Isthmian Canal authorities, in their wisdom, subject arrivals from Colombian ports to rigid quarantine. Indeed, so jealous are they of the newly-earned reputation of the canal zone for healthiness that as often as not communication with the shore at Cartagena may prevent one visiting the Panama Canal. On the eastern voyage, however, no such restrictions are involved, and as a rule several hours may be spent ashore more or less profitably at each of the ports, of which those most frequently visited are

203

Cartagena and Puerto Colombia, or Savanilla, in Colombia, and Puerto Cabello in Venezuela.

From Colon, the cosmopolitan town at the northern mouth of the great waterway which is to link the Atlantic to the Pacific, it is only a twenty-four hours' steam to Cartagena. Porto Bello, the scene of swash-buckling Admiral Vernon's victory in 1739, once strongly fortified but long since fallen from its high estate, is passed and the steamer goes near if not actually over the spot where the body of the redoubtable Drake was committed to the deep in 1596.

Long before Cartagena is seen the " Popa," an almost isolated hill which dominates it, comes into view; it is easy to appreciate how this eminence acquired its name, so closely does it resemble from a distance the poop of a ship. On one side, that nearest the town, the hill has only a gentle slope; but on the other it is exceedingly steep; on the summit are perched the white buildings of an old Augustinian monastery—Nuestra Señhora de la Popa. Cartagena itself stands on a sandy peninsula at the foot of the Popa, being connected with the continent by an artificial neck of land.

From the apparently exposed position of the city one might think that it would be possible to steam right up to it from the open sea; but nature has pro-tected it by reefs and the formidable Salmedina sand-bank which necessitates an approach by a circuitous route—for ships on the western voyage—along and round the islands which close in its magnificent harbour. This harbour or bay was once gained by two

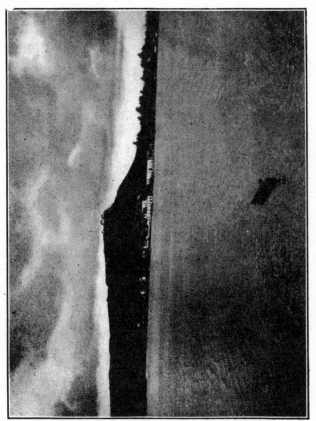

THE "POPA" FROM CARTAGENA HARBOUR

bocas or mouths, the Boca Grande quite near the town and the Boca Chica (the narrow mouth) many miles farther south ; but after an attack by Vernon in 1740 the Spaniards effectively closed the Boca Grande by sinking old vessels in the fairway. Over these the sand has collected, and now the Boca Chica alone is available for navigation.

So narrow is this entrance that no more than a single vessel can make use of it at a time, and not only could the proverbial biscuit be thrown to land as a steamer passes through, but a conversation could be easily maintained without raising the voice with any one on shore. On either side of the narrow mouth are forts which formerly helped to make Cartagena Harbour one of the safest anchorages in the New World. That on the right is Fort San José, while on the left is the once formidable Fort San Fernando.

After negotiating the narrow entrance, the steamer makes her way for about six or seven miles up the tortuous channel in the great landlocked harbour along the mangrove-covered shores of Tierra Bomba, which since the closing of the Boca Grande has been an island in name only. A small village is passed, then another fort protecting the anchorage where the galleons lay in the old days, and the steamer is warped alongside a wharf on the very spit of coral rock along which Drake made his successful attack on Cartagena, described below, and consequently called to this day " Drake's Spit."

On this historic spit a light railway now takes passengers to and from a small station outside the old city walls. The Cartagena terminus of the railway running to Calamar, which is beyond, furnishes a typical instance of the happy-go-lucky way in which the business of the less enlightened South American republics is conducted, for only the walls are standing, the roof never having been put on, and the appearance which it presents being in consequence most desolate. The town, which is extremely picturesque in spite of—or perhaps to some extent on account of—its dirt, is entered through an archway in the massive freestone walls which still encircle it and once made it almost impregnable. Then in a moment one is transported to old Spain. Here are houses bright with many colours of which blue and yellow prevail, with their roofed balconies and their cool patios. Here, too, are the graceful and olive-complexioned ladies of sunny Spain, though most are of a darker tint, all wearing the ubiquitous mantilla. Here again it behoves one to walk warily and to listen for the shout of " Alla va! Alla va! " if he would avoid a shower bath of slops, for Cartagena is innocent of any system of drainage, and the ill-paved streets are made the receptacle for all kinds of rubbish and worse.

The churches are many and noble as far as their architecture is concerned, but, alas, they are in a sad state of decay, and even the brick floor of the campanile of the cathedral shakes in an ominous way when one walks on it, the beams on which it is supported being eaten through and through. The interiors are tawdry, and there is little trace of lavish decorations with which they were adorned in the days when Cartagena was in its prime. The house of the Inquisition near the principal square is now the home of a prosperous merchant, and there is not much in the comfortably furnished rooms to remind one of the horrors which they witnessed when Cartagena was the chief seat of the Inquisition in the New World. In one of them, however, an old and worn railing is still pointed out behind which the victims stood when they received their sentence; afterwards they were hurried into a windowless chamber beyond, which doubtless resounded with screams of terror and of anguish. It is generally believed, too, that the cruel apparatus of the Inquisition lies buried below the patio, which, judging from the height of the palms in it, has not been disturbed for very many years.

It was on the eve of the national fêtes that the writer visited Cartagena. Throughout the town there was an air of suppressed excitement — suppressed because the celebration of the anniversary of the deliverance of Colombia by the great Bolivar was not to begin officially until evening. But it was easy to see that something was in the air. The public buildings were being decorated with the national colours and the streets were being prepared with feverish haste for dancing, which was to take place later in the day, while occasionally one of the younger generation of Colombians would relieve his pent-up feelings by the discharge of a squib.

At 5 o'clock the bells rang out from the towers of the cathedral and the old church of San Pedro and the fête had begun. An hour or so later pandemonium reigned throughout the town, carnival costumes had been donned and the respectable Cartagenians, wearing the weirdest of masks, were dancing in the square to the strains of the noisiest of brass bands. Fireworks were let off in all directions, and it is needless to say that the small party of English visitors were singled out for the attention of the squib throwers.

Later in the evening the crowds, headed by the band, moved off to one of the main streets where the dancing was continued with redoubled energy, while ladies wearing the traditional mantilla watched the scene from the picturesque balconies, making unconsciously a charming picture. All night long the strains of the band and the shouts of the revellers were wafted across the harbour, and day had broken before the sounds of revelry died away.

It was in 1572 that Sir Francis Drake, who sailed on May 24 from Plymouth in the *Pascha* of seventy tons, accompanied by his brother John Drake in the *Swan* of twenty-five tons, after raiding Nombre de Dios, determined to take Cartagena. On August 13 he dropped anchor off the two islands at the mouth of the harbour and entered the great lagoon in his boats. Near the entrance he found a frigate with only an old man in charge, and, ascertaining from him that the alarm had been given, he contented himself with capturing a ship from Seville of 240 tons burthen and two small frigates. Drake's force was a small one, and not having enough men in his own ships he decided that his brother's ship, the *Swan*, must be sacrificed. But she was considered a lucky vessel, and he knew

208

A CHARACTERISTIC STREET IN CARTAGENA

that her crew would not scuttle her, even if ordered to do so, so he sent carpenters on board at the dead of night with instructions to bore holes in her. This they did without any difficulty. Next morning Drake went on board and remarked that the vessel seemed to be rather low in the water. The crew then for the first time perceived that she was sinking and rushed to the pumps. Their efforts being, however, of no avail, they were easily persuaded to set fire to the ship and abandon her. Though his crew was thus strengthened Drake did not on this occasion persist in his attempt on Cartagena but withdrew to the Isthmus of Darien.

Thirteen years later—on September 12, 1585—he again left Plymouth with twenty-five sail and pinnaces, and a force of 2300 soldiers and sailors, the former being under the command of Lieut.-General Christopher Carleil, "a man of long experience in the warres as well by sea as land." After capturing St. Iago in the Cape Verde Islands, and after a successful attack on San Domingo, from whose inhabitants they took a ransom of 25,000 ducats, they put over to the Main or Tierra Firma and set their course for Cartagena. Their vessels drew little water; and, after coasting along the Main they passed so near the town that they were within reach of the culverins which defended it from attack on the sea side. At four o'clock in the afternoon the small fleet entered the harbour mouth, which "lay some three miles toward the westward of the towne"—presumably the Boca Grande—without meeting with any opposition. In the evening troops were landed under General Carleil near the Boca Grande and instructions were given to them to " march forwarde about midnight, as easily as foote might fall," along the sea shore, so that they might not lose their way as they did at first owing to the mistake of a guide—a mistake which cost them a few hours' much needed rest.

When they came within two miles of the town their presence was discovered and they were attacked by a body of cavalry numbering some hundreds. The ground was, however, covered with bushes which helped the invaders and hindered the horsemen, who, at the first volley from Drake's force, retired precipitately towards the town. Meanwhile Martin Frobisher, who was vice-admiral of the small fleet, opened fire on the fort at the entrance of the harbour, with the object of drawing attention from the invading party. The fort being strong and the harbour protected by a chain boom, they failed to effect an entrance, though on the other hand they incurred no loss beyond damage to the rudder of Frobisher's ship, which was hit by a saker shot.

The English troops were now on the march along the famous spit described above. " Halfe a myle behither the towne or lesse, the ground we were on grewe to bee straight, and not above fiftie paces over, having the main sea on the one side of it, and the harbour water or inner sea . . . on the other side."

The spit was defended by a stone wall and a ditch, with a single opening for the cavalry to pass through, which was protected with a barricade of wine-butts standing one on the other. The road was commanded by six pieces of ordnance, demi-culverins and sakers, and it was flanked by two great galleys with bows towards the shore mounting eleven guns. These galleys carried three or four hundred small shot, and three hundred shot and pikes were available on land to guard the position.

Under cover of the dark Carleil and his troops marched silently along the sea shore reserving their ammunition. On reaching the wall they formed up " with pikes roundly together " and rushed the opening at daybreak. Down went the butts and pell-mell came swords and pikes together after the delivery of a volley " even at the enemies' nose." The English troops had better armour and longer pikes than their adversaries, who were unable to resist the furious onslaught and were driven back. General Carleil with his own hands killed the chief ensign bearer of the Spaniards, who fought manfully to the end. The defenders were hotly pursued as far as the market place, where they made a short stand, but it was soon captured by the now victorious Drake, and the enemy were put to flight. Then it was found that the town had been abandoned, women and children having been hurried to places of safety in the country upon the first approach of the English. The streets were barricaded and entrenched and some little resistance was offered, Indian bowmen having been placed at various points of vantage, who fired " arrowes most villanously empoysoned, so as if they did but breake the skinne, the partie so touched died without great marvell: some they slew of our people with their arrowes: some they likewise mischieved to death with certaine pricks of small sticks sharply pointed, of a foote and a halfe long, the one ende put into the ground, the other empoysoned, sticking fast up." The English were now masters of the situation; Drake's ambition was realised.

Many deeds of valour were performed on that day, not the least of them being the capture of Alonso Bravo, Governor and Chief Commander of Cartagena, by Captain Goring. The English losses were few, and the success of the attack was, in no small measure, due to the fact that "every man, as well of one part as of another, came so willingly on to the service, as the enemie was not able to endure the furie of such hot assault."

Drake remained in Cartagena for six weeks, but his joy at taking the city was chastened by the sickness which overtook his troops. They suffered severely from fever and ague, and so great was the mortality that a proposed expedition to Nombre de Dios and thence overland to Panama had, for the time being, to be abandoned. Now that it is a generally accepted fact that mosquitoes convey the infection of malaria and other fevers it is interesting to note that the cause of sickness was attributed to "the evening or first night ayre, which they terme La Serena, wherein they say and hold very firme opinion, that who so is then abroad in the open ayre, shall certainly be infected to the death, not being of the Indian or naturall race of those countrey people: by holding their watch, our men were thus subjected to the infectious ayre."

212

This was the old idea that prevailed for several centuries, and even quite recently caused travellers to Rome to close railway carriage windows whilst they were crossing the Campagna near sundown to keep out the miasma, the mal'aria, or bad air, which they believed to be the origin of the fever malaria. How near the old-time adventurers were to discovering the real source of infection—the mosquito! From the appreciation of the fact that it is at sunset that fevers were contracted, it seems such a short step to the discovery that it is then that mosquitoes are on the war-path, and that it is the mosquitoes which are the source of infection.

Drake remained in Cartagena for about six weeks, and though the houses of the merchants were sacked and spoiled of household goods and merchandise, and a great part of the city was burnt, courtesies were shown between the victors and the vanquished, who were feasted and treated with kindness and favour. A ransom of 110,000 ducats was at last agreed upon and Drake left the town, withdrawing some of his troops to a priory near the harbour waterside. He claimed that this building was not covered by the ransom and exacted a further sum for it and the fort at the entrance of the inner harbour.

Whilst negotiations were proceeding the fleet moved down to the harbour mouth and took in a supply of fresh water from a well on the island of Cares, which appears to have been a delightful spot, planted with orange trees and orchards of fruit. After a stay of six weeks altogether they set sail at the end of

March, but returned for another eight or ten days owing to a ship, which they had captured at San Domingo, called 'The New Year's Gift' (so full was she of ordnance, hides and other spoil), springing a leak.

Scarcely less memorable than the capture of Cartagena by Drake was the successful assault on the city a hundred years later by the French under de Ponti.

De Ponti's forces comprised about 4658 men, embarked on board fourteen ships, and 700 buccaneers commanded by M. du Casse, Governor of San Domingo, who with two companies of negroes were carried by private ships of war.

The combined fleet dropped anchor before Cartagena on April 12, 1697, and throughout the night the city was bombarded by a French galliot—the first bomb vessel ever seen in the West Indies. On the 14th the attack was concentrated on the fort at Boca Chica, the narrow entrance to the harbour already described, which at this period had four bastions, mounting thirty-three guns, and was defended also by a dry ditch. Under the fire of the bomb vessel, troops were landed and marched to within a quarter of a league of the fort without opposition. Then on the advice of the buccaneers 3000 men cut their way through the bush in single file and took possession of the road leading from Cartagena to the fort. The alarm was now sounded, and after a short engagement a small village near the fort was seized and a few negro prisoners were taken.

Next morning the Spanish endeavoured to re-establish

communication with the fort by water, but the dug-out in which the attempt was made was captured and twenty more prisoners, including two monks, were captured. The latter gave some useful information regarding the state of the garrison, and one of them was sent back under a flag of truce to summon the Governor to surrender. The Governor's reply was a curt refusal, and a determined attack was consequently made on the fort. The negroes cleared the bush away, mortars and guns were brought up, and the artillery, troops and buccaneers, who proved to be excellent sharpshooters, opened fire at short range. Two boats endeavoured to throw supplies into the garrison, and the buccaneers in their efforts to stop them got so close under the walls that they were able to prevent the garrison using their guns, killing every man who made his appearance.

The grenadiers were thus enabled to reach the draw-bridge, and scaling ladders had already been placed against the walls when Don Francisco Ximenes, the Governor, hoisted a white flag and offered to capitulate. Being told that they must surrender as prisoners of war, the garrison threw their arms over the ramparts and opened the gates of the fort. The French then took possession, securing 100 of the defenders, whom they made prisoners in a chapel.

On the following day, April 17, the fleet sailed into the spacious harbour, and the cowardly Spaniards in consternation set fire to their own ships to prevent their being captured by the enemy.

M. de Ponti now offered favourable terms to the

Governor of Cartagena, who replied that he was not lacking in guns, men or courage to defend the place, and that he was determined to do his duty.

The buccaneers then crossed the harbour to attack the monastery of the Popa and to occupy the heights and main roads. Their task was an easy one for they found it abandoned, the monks having left shortly before with all their valuables.

Meanwhile the main army marched on the fort of Santa Cruz, and though that position mounted sixty guns, was surrounded by a moat, and was accessible only from the land side, where the mud was knee-deep, the garrison surrendered without firing a shot. Fort San Lazaro was next singled out for attack, and while de Ponti maintained a conference with the garrison, his men surrounded the fort. Roads were cut on the face of the hill, and the buccaneers again showed their skill as sharpshooters, picking off the Spaniards with such precision that they were forced to abandon the fort in disorder and retire into the city.

Selecting a position behind Fort San Lazaro as the base of their operations, the French then made active preparations for besieging the city. Batteries were erected and artillery landed, and for several days a hot cannonade was maintained by the bomb vessel in the roads and the mortars on shore.

Then came the news that Indians were advancing to the assistance of the besieged. Three hundred and fifty buccaneers were in consequence detailed to watch them, and these men, delighted no doubt at having an opportunity for plunder, ravaged the country round for a distance of several leagues and returned with fifty prisoners and much booty.

On April 28 and 29 a vigorous cannonade was maintained and on the 30th the fire from all the batteries was directed against a breach which had been made in the walls. M. du Casse, in spite of a wound from which he was suffering, led the grenadiers forward and they were followed by the buccaneers and the rest of the army. Many fell killed and wounded by the fire from the bastion of Santa Catarina and the survivors fought their way to the breach, which was defended with great courage by the Spaniards, who had the advantage of being armed with lances longer than the weapons of their adversaries.

The siege was kept up with vigour until May 2, when the garrison was reduced to such straits by the combined fire from the land side and from the *Sceptre* and the *Vermandois* which were lying in the roads that the Spaniards were forced to capitulate.

M. du Casse entered the city to arrange the terms of capitulation, but the Governor would only treat with M. de Ponti. On May 3 terms were eventually agreed upon, the Governor with the troops and militia being allowed to march out with drums beating, matches lighted and two pieces of cannon. No damage was to be done to the churches, all state property was to be handed over to M. de Ponti, the inhabitants were to be permitted to leave the city with their clothes and money and slaves according to their rank, and those who chose to remain under the obedience of His Most Christian Majesty were to enjoy the

217

same privileges, rights and immunities which they enjoyed under his Catholic Majesty and were to be left in peaceable possession of their goods with the exception of gold, silver, and precious stones.

As soon as the articles were signed a detachment of buccaneers was to share with the troops the duty of defending the city, and both sailors and soldiers were forbidden to enter the houses under pain of death.

On May 4 the Governor marched out and de Ponti, entering Cartagena, attended a solemn service in the cathedral, where a solemn Te Deum was chanted. The inhabitants then brought in their money and valuables, while the victors gave themselves up to the wildest dissipation. Every article of the capitulation was broken. The churches were plundered and the women violated, and the soldiers committed every kind of excess. The result was that 800 perished in six days, and the French had soon to abandon all hopes of keeping the place. They therefore shipped the plunder and 86 brass guns from the batteries, and after blowing up the forts of San Lazaro and Boca Chica took their departure.

M. du Casse had meanwhile demanded from de Ponti the share of the plunder to which he and his adventurers were entitled. Great was the indignation of the buccaneers when he was informed that it amounted to 40,000 dollars only. They expected far more, and being determined to get it, returned to the unfortunate city. Rounding up all the men they could find they locked them in the cathedral and demanded 5,000,000 dollars as ransom for their lives.

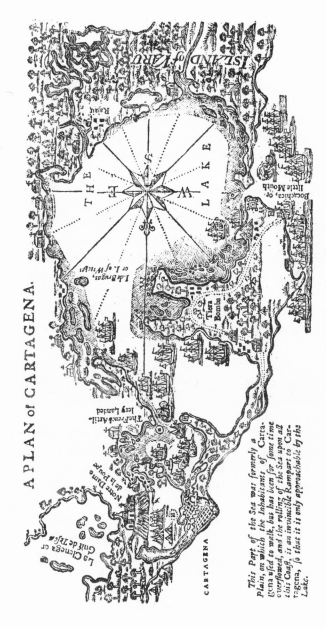

A PLAN of CARTAGENA.

La Cienega or Gulf de Tesfa

Notre Dame de la Poupe

The French Artillery Landed

CARTAGENA

L.de Brugas, or I. of Witches

Rajin

ISLAND of VARU

THE LAKE

S

E W

Tiera Bomba

Bocachica, or little Mouth

This Part of the Sea was formerly a Plain, on which the Inhabitants of Cartagena used to walk, but has been for some time overflowed, and the rolling of the Sea upon all this Coast, is an invincible Rampart to Cartagena, so that it is only approachable by the Lake.

AN OLD PLAN OF CARTAGENA

More than a million dollars were at once brought in, and after remaining four days the buccaneers decamped, having first divided the silver and gold, which amounted to a thousand crowns a man. They decided to divide up the merchandise when they arrived at the island of La Vache. Their intentions were, however, doomed to be frustrated, for the marauders had only proceeded about thirty leagues when they fell in with the combined English and Dutch fleets, which made short work of them.

One of their vessels, *Le Christ*, well laden with money, was captured by the Dutch, another, the *Cerf Volant*, equally rich in plunder was taken by the English, a third was driven ashore at San Domingo and burnt, while a fourth was chased back to Cartagena, where her crew was captured and made to work in the rebuilding of the fortifications which the men themselves had helped to destroy.

Five other vessels managed to reach San Domingo; but the treasure which they contained was subsequently taken by an English squadron which captured Petit Gouyave in that island. For his services du Casse was decorated with the Cross of St. Louis, and orders were eventually sent out for 1,400,000 livres of the treasure taken by de Ponti to be distributed among the free-booters to whom the successful capture of Cartagena on this occasion was mainly due.

Admiral Vernon, the "hero" of Porto Bello, was the next Englishman to attack Cartagena. Known to his men as "Old Grog"—a nickname which he earned from his habit of wearing a boat cloak made of grogram—it was he who put a stop to the practice of serving out raw rum to the sailors, causing a mixture of rum and water to be substituted for it, a concoction which has ever since been called grog. For this beneficial move he was perhaps more deserving of fame than for his assault on Cartagena; his attempt to take the city ended altogether disastrously.

Vernon, who had seen active service off the Spanish Main under Commodore Wager, was a member of the House of Commons in 1739. In that capacity he was constantly accusing our officers of cowardice in not attacking Porto Bello, and he openly boasted that he could take the place with six ships. He was arrogant and boastful to a degree, but he had a considerable following of supporters and the ministry determined that he should be given an opportunity of showing his prowess. They accordingly raised him to the rank of Vice-Admiral of the Fleet, and placed under his command four 70-gun ships, three 60's, and a 50-gun frigate.

With this squadron he sailed on August 3. When off Cadiz he detached three ships to search for a fleet of treasure galleons, and proceeded with the remainder to Porto Bello. The works of this place were strong, but the Governor made a very poor defence. On November 20 the fleet anchored off the Iron Castle, which was successfully stormed. The Castles of St. Ieronimo and Gloria above it still held out, and preparations were made to reduce them, but, on the following day, the Spanish Governor surrendered them without a shot being fired.

The news of the victory was received with the greatest enthusiasm in England. Bonfires were lighted and medals innumerable were struck, bearing on the obverse a figure representing the admiral, with the palm of victory by his side and the inscription, " British glory revived by Admiral Vernon," and, on the reverse, six ships and three forts, with the following words round them : " He took Porto Bello with six ships only. November 22, 1739." Others were inscribed, " By courage and conduct." Many public-houses, too, were re-christened after the hero of Porto Bello.

After blowing up the forts and castles Vernon proceeded to Jamaica, and on February 25 in the following year he sailed from Port Royal with twenty-nine ships, a squadron of frigates and transports and 12,000 troops for the reduction of Cartagena.

On March 9 the fleet engaged the forts of St. Iago and San Felipe and soldiers were landed. They suffered severely from the fire of the shore batteries and were prevented from following up their success by the refusal of Vernon, whose head was quite turned by his victory at Porto Bello, to co-operate with General Wentworth, who had command of the troops. On March 24 and 25 further successes were gained, but it was not until March 30 that the harbour was entered and preparations were made for an attack on Fort San Lazaro, whose crumbling redoubts can still be seen among trees and bush at the foot of the Popa. The troops made a furious assault on the fort, but they were repulsed again and again, and on April 14 the siege was raised.

OLD CARTAGENA

The English force in this disastrous expedition was reduced to 3000 by wounds and sickness. It was claimed that Wentworth could have cut off the town, but to such lengths did Vernon's jealousy go, that he was denied the supplies of food and water by the ships, which were essential to the well-being of the troops and to the success of the undertaking.

This was the last attack made upon Cartagena by a foreign adversary. The subsequent history of the city has been mainly one of those political agitations and revolutions which seem inseparable from South American countries. In 1815 the town was captured by the great liberator Bolivar; but it was regained by the royalists in the same year. The republicans again took Cartagena six years later, and since the year 1821 its independence has not been challenged.

CHAPTER X

A BARBADOS MYSTERY

On an eminence above Oistin's, a small hamlet at the head of the bay of the same name on the south coast of Barbados, stands the parish church of Christ Church. It was built from designs of Captain Senhouse, R.N., to replace an earlier structure which was destroyed by the hurricane in 1831, and, although it is worthy of attention from the fact that in many respects it is said to resemble a ship, it is in the churchyard surrounding it that the chief interest lies.

Between the years 1812 and 1820 a series of remarkable events took place there, the real cause of which has never to this day been satisfactorily explained. At the time they occasioned among the negro population of the island a feeling of consternation which was only equalled in intensity by the mystification of the white inhabitants.

Though the salient features of the several versions of the "Barbados Coffin Story" are the same, the details vary greatly. To such an extent, indeed, has the story been twisted and turned about to suit the styles of individual writers and the tastes of their readers, that it is difficult to winnow the true grain of fact from the chaff of descriptive colouring. It is probable, however,

224

that a recently unearthed manuscript of the late
Hon. Nathan Lucas, grandfather of the Rev. Charles
Kingsley, now furnishes the only really dependable
account. This manuscript, which is in the possession of
Mr. Edward T. Racker, of Barbados, was brought to
light by Mr. Forster M. Alleyne, who has devoted much
time to proving, as he has now successfully done beyond
fear of contradiction, that the coffin story is actually
based on fact; and inasmuch as Mr. Nathan Lucas, a
respected member of the Legislative Council, was an
eye-witness of one of the scenes in the churchyard, his
statements which were attested by the Rev. Thomas D.
Orderson, D.D., Rector of the parish, may, at any rate,
be accepted as authentic.

The vault where the remarkable occurrences which
will now be described took place belonged at one time
to the Adams Castle Estate, formerly the property of the
Walrond family from whom it passed to the Elliotts.
Constructed of massive blocks of stone quarried from the
local coral, it was cemented together so firmly that it
looked as if it were hewn out of the solid rock. For
better security against hurricanes, and owing also to
some extent to the nature of the foundations, the vault
was built partly above and partly below the level of the
ground. Within, the sides sloped inwards towards the
top, the arched roof being consequently smaller than
the base, which measured twelve feet long by six and a
half feet broad. The entrance was closed by a ponderous slab of blue Devonshire marble which rested
against the sloping side, and the interior was reached by
several steps.

For many years no one was buried in the vault; but in July 1807 the rector was asked to allow the remains of a Mrs. Thomasina Goddard to be placed in it. The necessary permission having been granted, the funeral took place on the 31st of the month. On February 22, in the following year, when the vault was opened to receive the leaden coffin of Mary Anna Maria Chase, the infant daughter of the Hon. Thomas Chase, Mrs. Goddard's coffin was in its proper place, and nothing unusual seemed to have happened. When, however, the vault was again unsealed on July 6, 1812, on the occasion of the funeral of Dorcas Chase, another daughter of the Hon. Thomas Chase, all was confusion within. To the utter amazement of the funeral party, the coffins of Mrs. Goddard and Mary Chase were found to have been violently disturbed, that of the infant being head downwards in the opposite corner of the vault to the one in which it had been placed. The funeral ceremony was, however, proceeded with, and the vault was once more hermetically sealed, the disturbance being attributed to the mischievous act of some of the negro labourers who attended the previous interment. Nothing further of importance appears to have taken place in connection with the vault until four years later, though the Hon. Thomas Chase was himself laid to rest in it on August 9, 1812. On September 25, 1816, it was again opened, this time for the reception of the coffin of Samuel Brewster Ames, another infant. When the stone was removed, the labourers were horrified to find that the coffins were again disarranged. Suspicion once more rested on the men; but they stoutly

THE MYSTERIOUS VAULT, CHRIST CHURCH, BARBADOS

protested their innocence, and the coffins having been replaced in their former positions, the vault closed. Little else was now talked of in the island than the coffin affair at Christ Church. The negroes on the one hand were convinced that the disturbance was due to "jumbies" or "duppies," the ghosts, of which they have a pious horror, while the white population with equal certainty attributed it to the mischievous pranks of some practical jokers. The affair continued to be a constant topic of discussion, and interest in it had by no means died out when on November 17, 1816, the body of Samuel Brewster, who had been murdered during the insurrection of the slaves in the preceding April, was removed to the vault from St. Philip, where it first lay. Crowds flocked to the churchyard and, from a respectful distance, watched the opening of the tomb. The ponderous stone was slid aside, and it was at once seen that there had been a repetition of the former disturbances. Mrs. Goddard's coffin had fallen to pieces, but the leaden coffins which were still whole were again in a state of much confusion and disorder. All efforts to elucidate the mystery having failed, the remains of the wooden coffin were tied in a bundle and were placed between the elder Miss Clarke's coffin and the wall. The leaden coffins were then restored to their proper places, and the slab was again firmly cemented over the entrance.

Thousands visited the churchyard to see the mysterious vault, and the excitement throughout the length and breadth of the island became so intense that the Governor, Lord Combermere, decided to be present at an interment—that of Thomasina Clarke—on July 7, 1819.

He accordingly went to the churchyard, attended by his aides-de-camp. The vault was again opened, and for the fourth time the leaden coffins were discovered to be in a state of confusion, though the remains of Mrs. Goddard's coffin were undisturbed. The Governor immediately caused every part of the floor to be sounded to ascertain whether any subterranean passage or entrance was concealed. It was, however, found to be perfectly firm and solid, and not even a crack was to be seen. All attempts to solve the mystery failed. The displaced coffins were re-arranged, and after the mourners had left, the floor was carefully sanded with white sand, with the object of tracing any movements however slight. The door was slid into its wonted place, and secured with new cement, on which the Governor made several impressions with his own seal, while many of those present added various private marks. The party then withdrew. Interest in the strange affair was maintained, and the re-opening of the vault was eagerly awaited.

Then came the scene of which Mr. Nathan Lucas was an eye-witness. On April 18, 1820, Lord Combermere was staying with Mr. Robert Bowcher Clarke at Eldridge's Plantation, next to Christ Church, and at noon, when the negroes were returning from the field, conversation turned upon the vault. After an animated discussion it was suggested that a visit should be paid to the churchyard. This was no sooner said than done. Taking with them eight or ten of the negroes, the party, which consisted of the Governor, Mr. R. Bowcher Clarke, Mr. Rowland Cotton and the Hon. Nathan

A BARBADOS MYSTERY

SKETCHES OF THE CHASE VAULT

From the manuscript of the Hon. Nathan Lucas

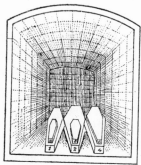

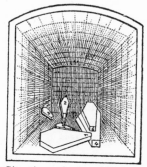

Situation of the Coffins when the Vault was closed July 7, 1819

in the presence of the Reverend Thomas H. Orderson

Situation of the Coffins on April 18, 1820, when the Vault was reopened

in the presence of the Rt. Hble. Lord Combermere, R. B. Clarke, Esq., Rowland Cotton, and Honble. N. Lucas

July 6, 1812.   *Dorcas Chase ; leaden coffin, No.* 1.

August 9, 1812.   *Honble. Thomas Chase ; leaden coffin, No.* 2.

September 25, 1816.   *S. B. Ames; infant; leaden coffin, No.* 3.

November 17, 1816.   *Samuel Brewster, shot in the Insurrection, April* 15 *; his remains removed to the Vault, November* 17 *; leaden coffin, No.* 4.

February 22, 1818 [? 1808].   *A. M. Chase; infant; leaden coffin, No.* 5.

July 7, 1819.   *Thomasina Clarke ; wooden coffin, No.* 6.

Certified,

T. H. ORDERSON, D.D.,
Rector of the Parish of Christ Church.

On the side of Number 4 there were the remains of an old wooden coffin tied up between the wall and the coffin, and these were found in their original situation when the vault was opened in 1820.
T. H. ORDERSON.

The coffins had been moved twice before their last inspection.
T. H. O.

Lucas, repaired to the churchyard. The Rev. Thomas Orderson, D.D., Rector of the parish, was sent for and soon appeared on the scene, while the party was further reinforced by Major the Hon. J. Finch, the Governor's Military Secretary and A.D.C. On arrival at the vault, everything was to all outward appearance just as it had been left on July 7 in the preceding year. Indeed, not a stone appeared to have been touched, and as no one but the members of the small party themselves were aware of this visit to the churchyard, which was made on the spur of the moment, collusion or deception was impossible. The structure was closely examined on all sides. Everything seemed to be secure. The cement was uncracked and the large impressions of the Governor's seal were as sharp and as perfect as on the day on which they were made, the cement being now as hard as stone. Each person present who on the former occasion had made his private mark, satisfied himself that it had not been tampered with. Orders were then given for the removal of the slab. The cement was with difficulty broken and pressure was brought to bear upon the stone, but the united efforts of the labourers failed at first to move it. A hush fell on the spectators. Then a renewed attempt was made and at last the marble responded to the efforts of the panting negroes and yielded a few inches. By degrees it was moved aside sufficiently to enable one of the party to enter the vault. The reason for the failure to move the stone at the first attempt was not far to seek. Resting against it on the inside was one of the massive leaden coffins— a coffin which took several men's united strength to

230

move—standing upside down! And yet there were no footprints in the sand! Small wonder then that the opinion prevailing among the negroes was that the disturbances were due to supernatural agency.

So superstitious did the people now become through this latest manifestation that it was decided that the vault should be closed, and shortly afterwards the coffins which it contained were removed and buried elsewhere in the churchyard in separate graves. The vault was abandoned, and has never since been used. It now stands deserted and forlorn, and if curiosity prompts him to enter it the visitor will find nothing inside except, perhaps, some stray leaves and a few bones which have been thrown there at some later date.

To his manuscript account the Hon. Nathan Lucas appended the following memorandum signed by the Rector, the Rev. T. H. Orderson, D.D., which may, perhaps, assist the curious in clearing up a mystery, the true key to which has not as yet been found:

"In England, at this day, the body is first enclosed in a shell; that in lead, and lastly, the Coffin of State without all, ornamented, etc. In Barbados, it is otherwise; the body is put at once into a Coffin of State, etc., and that is inclosed in lead, at the grave, and is without the wooden coffin. The children's coffins were placed upon bricks in the vault. Mr. Chase's on the rock, the bottom of the Vault. Now how could one of the *leaden* coffins be set upon end against the wall? Why were the coffins of wood *in situ*? and why was the bundle of Mrs. Goddard's decayed coffin found where it had been left? Wood certainly would first float.

There was no vestige of water to be discovered in the vault; no marks where it had been; and the vault is in a level churchyard, by no means in a fall much less in a run of water. Earthquake could not have done this without levelling the churchyard to the ground. Being informed some time after that a similar occurrence had been said to have happened in England, I had the account looked for, and the following copy was given to me; I did not see the work from whence it was extracted, but I have no reason to doubt the accuracy of it.

"'From the *European Magazine* for September, 1815— 'The Curious Vault at Stanton in Suffolk. On opening it some years since, several *leaden* coffins, with wooden cases, that had been fixed on biers, were found displaced to the great astonishment of many inhabitants of the village. The coffins were placed as before, and properly closed: when some time ago, another of the family dying, they were a second time found displaced; and two years after, they were not only found all off the biers, but one coffin as heavy as to require eight men to raise it was found on the fourth step that leads into the vault.' Whence arose this operation, in which it is certain no one had a hand? N.B.—It was occasioned by water, as is imagined, though no sign of it appeared at the different periods of time that the vault was opened. The following is the statement of Mr. Lucas as regards the Christ Church Vault. 'I examined the walls, the arch and every part of the vault, and found every part old and similar; and a mason in my presence struck every part of the bottom with his hammer, and all was solid. I confess myself at a loss to account for the

A VIEW OF MONTEGO BAY, JAMAICA, FROM SPRING HILL

(See page 234)

movements of these *leaden* coffins. Thieves certainly
had no hand in it; and as for any practical wit or hoax,
too many were requisite to be trusted with the secret
for it to remain unknown; and as for negroes having
anything to do with it, their superstitious fear of the
dead and everything belonging to them preclude any
idea of the kind.—All I know is that it happened, and
that I was an eye-witness of the fact ! ! !"

Sir Robert Schomburgk briefly tells the coffin story
in his " History of Barbados"; Lady Combermere,
inspired by an anonymous pamphlet entitled "Death
Deeds," refers to it in her Life of her husband, and
Mr. Robert Reece contributed an account of it to
the pages of *Once a Week*. None of these writers
attempts, however, to solve the mystery. Mr. Andrew
Lang told of a similar disturbance of coffins which
is said to have occurred on the island of Oesel in the
Baltic; but he could give no explanation of it.

CHAPTER XI

THE LEGEND OF ROSE HALL

THE traveller who arrives at Montego Bay before sunset is fortunate. After the long and tiring journey across Jamaica by rail, the bright little town, approached through fields of waving sugar-cane, looks quite enchanting, with the blue sea beyond studded with the small islets called the Bogue Islands. Montego Bay—the name is derived from "manteca" or hogs-butter, the export of lard having once been the principal industry —is the chief tourist centre on the north coast of Jamaica. Every winter visitors flock to it from America in search of warmth and sunshine, which they never fail to find there in abundance. The town and district offer many attractions, not the least of which is the drive to Rose Hall, the haunted "Great House" on the estate of the same name. This place is, so it is said, haunted by the ghostly form of a notorious Mrs. Palmer, the wife of the Hon. John Palmer and owner of the neighbouring estate of Palmyra, whose life was characterised by wickedness and depravity unparalleled in the history of Jamaica.

Rose Hall stands on gently rising ground overlooking the sea, ten miles to the east of Montego Bay, from which it is reached by the great coast road which

ROSE HALL, JAMAICA

encircles Jamaica. The route to it lies past many charming little villas, an old fort, and the superb bathing place which is the pride and joy of the people of Montego Bay and is known as Doctor's Cave. Beyond these are the sugar estates of Providence and Iron Shore, with their works standing in a sea of sugar canes, while on either side at intervals are tall coco-nut palms which, judging from their size and appearance, must have stood there in the days when the carriages of the wealthy residents of Montego Bay clattered to and from the Rose Hall on the occasion of the merry parties and routs which were given there. Where the road actually fringes the shore the seaside grape is conspicuous, while occasional negro huts are the only residences discernible. Then Rose Hall, once the finest "Great House" or estates proprietor's residence in the West Indies, comes into view. Standing in a commanding situation it is dignified and stately, though now bereft of its two wings and fast falling into decay. As it is typical of the noble residences of the wealthy sugar lords of olden days, the following description of the house given by Hakewill in 1825 is of interest: "Rose Hall, the property and residence of John Rose Palmer, Esq., is situated on the seaside, at nearly equal distance from Montego Bay and Falmouth. The house of which we give a view is justly considered as the best in Jamaica, and was erected about fifty years since by the uncle of the present proprietor, at the expense of £30,000 sterling. It is placed at a delightful elevation, and commands a very extensive sea view. Its general appearance has much of the character of a handsome Italian villa. A double flight of stone steps leads to an open portico, giving access to the entrance hall ; on the left of which is the eating-room, and on the right the drawing-room, behind which are other apartments for domestic uses. The right wing, fitted up with great elegance, and enriched with painting and gilding, was the private apartment of the late Mrs. Palmer, and the left wing is occupied as servants' apartments and offices. The principal staircase, in the body of the house, is a specimen of joinery in mahogany and other costly woods seldom excelled, and leads to a suite of chambers in the upper story.

" This estate, and the adjoining one of Palmyra, descended to the present proprietor from his great uncle. Rose Hall estate has about 200 acres in canes, about the same quantity in grass, and about 250 in ruinate ; the Negro grounds are on Palmyra estate, which is a more seasonable situation.

" Palmyra estate contains about 1250 acres. The produce is shipped at a wharf at about two miles and a half distance. On the two estates are 252 negroes, and 276 head of cattle."

In the year 1868 Mr. Castello described the building in the following terms : " The first thing that strikes you is its size and magnitude ; the next, the imposing appearance of the flight of steps leading to the main entrance of the mansion. These are fourteen feet high, built of large square stones (hewn), and so arranged that the landing place serves as a portico, 20 feet square. A few brass stanchions curiously wrought and

twisted, serve to show what the railing had been, but
the few remaining are tarnished with verdigris, and
broken, bruised and turned in every direction. Magnificent, massive folding doors of solid mahogany four
inches thick with panels formed by the carver's chisel,
in many a scroll and many a device, are upheld by
brazen hinges which, fashioned like huge sea-monsters,
seem to bite the posts on which they hang. These
doors are in front of the main hall, a room of lofty
dimensions and magnificent proportions, a hall forty
feet long, thirty feet wide, and eighteen feet high,
formed of the same costly materials as the doors,
carved in the same manner out of solid planks, and
fashioned in curious and antique forms, while the top is
ornamented with a very deep cornice, formed after
the arabesque pattern. The floor is of the same expression and highly polished wood. Three portraits in
richly carved frames and painted by a master hand
immediately attract attention ; indeed, they are almost
the sole occupants of this lofty room, for of furniture there is scarcely a vestige, and the fine dark
coloured woods of the floor, base and doors, once so
highly polished are now damp and mouldy. The
gilding which formerly adorned the frames is now
tarnished and dull, but the pictures themselves are
fresh and fair, and the colours are as bright and vivid
as the day they came from the painter's easel. They
form a strange contrast to the neglect and decay of all
around, and carry the mind back to the time when
their originals lived in the old mansion ; when that
noble hall was filled with guests, when the song and

dance went gaily on, when instead of damp, mould and decay, all was bright and gorgeous, and India's riches glittered in profusion round the now bare and mouldering walls. One of these portraits represents a hard and stern-featured man, clothed in the scarlet and ermined robes of a judge. Another is of a mild, benevolent-looking, gentlemanly person dressed in the fashion of the olden times, with powdered hair, lace cravat, ruffles and shirt bosom, silk stockings and buckles, small clothes, brocaded vest and velvet coat. The third is a female of about five or six and twenty, and, if the painter has not flattered her, she must have been of exquisite beauty. Like the raven's wing is her hair, the latter falling in thick clustering ringlets unconfined by comb down over her alabaster neck and shoulders of purest white, her brow high and commanding, her eyes are dark and expressive, a smile plays sweetly round her rosy lips, and the expression of her countenance is pleasant, but at the same time her eye and brow show great determination of character. She is dressed in bridal robes; a wreath of orange-flowers round that fair high brow contrasts well with her dark locks, while her hand, that small, fairy-like hand, is in the act of putting aside the large bridal veil thrown loosely over her person. The frame of another picture is there, but the picture itself is gone. On the right side of this hall are two doors leading into bed-rooms. In the further one is an old-fashioned bedstead, made of ebony, with tall posts and very low feet. The wood is quite black and old, but very elaborately carved. This is the only object of interest. The rest

ROSE HALL, ST. JAMES, JAMAICA, IN 1825

From the engraving by Sutherland after the painting by James Hakewill

of the furniture is simple and modern. Examining closely the floor of the dressing room, we find the remains of a door which led to a subterranean passage, but the passage has long since been filled up, and the door is firmly closed. Directly opposite to the main door are two others fashioned in the same costly and expensive manner, which lead into another hall of rather smaller dimensions than the banqueting hall, one end of which is entirely occupied by a magnificent staircase, which still remains, and, though neglected and mouldy, seems to show what the rest of the mansion must have been. Everything about it, rails, balustrades and mouldings, is carved out of sandal wood. So highly polished and exquisitely designed is this piece of architecture that a late Governor-General offered a large sum, five hundred pounds, for the staircase as it stood, to be taken down and sent to England. This staircase leads to the upper rooms, eight in number, but these, though well proportioned, seem small in comparison with the rooms below. From each end of the portico, which extends the whole length of the back of the house, ran in semicircular shape two suites of rooms each three in number. Those on the right side have all decayed and fallen to ruin, and you can only trace their foundations; those on the left are still entire, though supported by many a prop, while the yawning walls and gaping floors show the time of their fall is not far distant. The first of these rooms was a billiard room, the second was devoted to music, and the third and farther from the house was a bedroom. These rooms were fitted up in the European style, with hangings, and plastered; and consequently exhibit in a greater degree, by the broken plaster and fluttering paper, the desolation and ruin of the whole place, than the other apartments that are all ceiled with wood. The bed-chamber still has some of its furniture remaining, a handsome bed-stead, old-fashioned, low, quaintly carved, with ebony inlaid with other woods still remains standing tottering in one corner; these with a few broken chairs, serve to show that time, not the robber, has been the spoiler here."

Time and the tropical climate, assisted by the active hand of the vandal, have since played havoc with Rose Hall. The entrance gates have gone, and by one of the pillars on which they used to hang lies an old-time gun which defended the house from pirates and other marauders. The slope leading up to the main entrance is closely overgrown with bush. Over the rail-less steps a wild orange tree has spread its branches, compelling the visitor to stoop low before he can ascend to a portico commanding an extensive view of cane pieces, and coco-nut avenues, which Mr. and Mrs. Palmer once enjoyed. The brass fittings have been removed from the still massive doors, and the grand entrance hall is now bare save for one or two crude oil paintings propped against the walls and perhaps a few bags of pimento, to such base uses has it now been put. Beyond the spacious hall is the inner hall with its famous staircase, for which the owner —to his credit be it said—refused a most tempting offer made by a Governor of Jamaica who was so

THE ROSA PALMER MONUMENT IN THE PARISH CHURCH
AT MONTEGO BAY, JAMAICA

charmed by it that he wanted to acquire it for his
residence in Ireland; and on either side are the
reception rooms. Upstairs, the work of destruction
has, alas, proceeded further. In many parts the
roof of this fine old house has given way, and the
windows are—horrible as it may seem—fastened with
that abomination of the tropics, "tin-roofing." On
the floor of Mrs. Palmer's room, what are alleged to be
blood stains are still pointed out though it has been
conclusively proved that the tragedy connected for so
many years by tradition with Rose Hall really took
place several miles away. Of the two wings, few traces
now remain beyond the massive foundations, which
time has failed to shatter; but the kitchen, which like
all West Indian kitchens stands away from the house,
has been protected by a temporary roof, and the
immense fireplace and oven—into which it is said that
Mrs. Palmer frequently put the remains of her victims
—are still a source of interest.

This then is the house which for nearly a century
has borne the reputation of being haunted. On
more than one occasion the ghostly form of Mrs. Ann
Palmer is said to have been seen moving up the great
staircase, and visitors who have had the courage to
pass a night in the Hall have been thrown violently
from their beds and nearly smothered with their
mattresses. Again, the story goes that a white figure
of a woman, which made its sudden appearance with
beckoning hand on the road between the Hall and
Montego Bay, so terrified the horses of Mr. Palmer's
carriage that they bolted for many miles into the inn

yard in Montego Bay, while Mr. Palmer himself was so terrified that he collapsed and died of fever shortly afterwards. Artificers and workmen, too, complained of their work being interrupted by a woman in white—this always happens in ghost stories—but it does not appear that the Psychical Society has ever taken serious cognisance of these supernatural happenings.

Now in the picturesque old Parish Church of Montego Bay there is a handsome monument to "Rosa Palmer, wife of the Hon. John Palmer," by the eminent sculptor John Bacon. It represents a female figure leaning over an urn, and the circumstance that there is a blue vein (a flaw in the marble) near her neck—suggestive of strangulation—led to the common belief that the Mrs. Palmer, whose memory it perpetuates, was the profligate mistress of Rose Hall, who met with a violent death. The monument was, however, really erected in honour of Mr. John Palmer's first wife, whose virtues are thus touchingly recorded:

NEAR THIS PLACE
ARE DEPOSITED THE REMAINS OF
Mrs. ROSA PALMER,
WHO DIED ON THE FIRST DAY OF MAY, 1790.
HER MANNERS WERE OPEN, CHEERFUL AND AGREEABLE,
AND BEING BLESSED WITH A
PLENTIFUL FORTUNE, HOSPITALITY
DWELT WITH HER AS LONG AS
HEALTH PERMITTED HER TO
ENJOY SOCIETY.

THE LEGEND OF ROSE HALL

EDUCATED BY THE ANXIOUS CARE OF A
REVEREND DIVINE, HER FATHER,
HER CHARITIES WERE NOT OSTENTATIOUS BUT
OF A NOBLER KIND;
SHE WAS WARM IN HER ATTACHMENTS TO HER FRIENDS
AND GAVE THE MOST SIGNAL PROOF OF IT
IN THE LAST MOMENTS OF HER LIFE.
THIS TRIBUTE OF AFFECTION AND RESPECT
IS ERECTED BY HER HUSBAND,
THE HONOURABLE JOHN PALMER,
AS A MONUMENT OF HER WORTH
AND OF HIS GRATITUDE.
BACON, SCULPTOR, 1794.

In the churchyard a stone marking the place where this Mrs. Palmer was actually buried is inscribed:

UNDERNEATH THIS STONE
ARE DEPOSITED THE REMAINS OF
ROSA PALMER,
WIFE OF THE HONOURABLE JOHN PALMER,
OF THIS PARISH,
ON THE FIRST DAY OF MAY, 1790.
AGED 72 YEARS.

This much malinged Mrs. Palmer, who was the daughter of the Rev. John Kelly, the "pious divine" mentioned in the inscription, was married successively to Mr. Henry Fanning, Mr. George Ash, and Mr. Norwood Witter before she was led to the altar by the Hon. John Palmer in 1767. She appears to have been a lady of exemplary character and altogether beyond reproach.

The same cannot be said of the *second* Mrs. Palmer, whose evil reputation is associated with Rose Hall. This lady was an Irish immigrant who had been introduced into Jamaica under the terms of the law which compelled each estate's proprietor to leaven his holding of African slaves with a certain proportion of white servants or, failing that, to pay a heavy fine. That she was attractive seems to be beyond doubt, for, like her namesake, she had been three times married before she became the wife of the widowed John Palmer and the mistress of Rose Hall. What the fate of her first three husbands was history does not relate, but subsequent events justified the belief that they did not die in their beds, and it is extremely likely that Mr. Palmer would have shared their fate if she had survived, for on a ring she wore were the ominous words :

" If I survive I shall have five."

Many and terrible were the misdeeds of this woman whose cruelty to her slaves became a byword in the district. Overcome by jealousy at the attentions paid by her step-son to a young and pretty negress she brought false accusations against the girl, who was taken before the plantation court, consisting of two magistrates and three freeholders, which—remarkable as it may seem—had power to pass sentences of death or of bodily mutilation. The result was that the girl was beheaded. Even this did not satisfy the morbid tastes

THE SPACIOUS ENTRANCE HALL, ROSE HALL, JAMAICA

of Mrs. Palmer, who preserved the head in spirits, and used to invite visitors to "look at the pretty creature."

Many were the stories told of how passers-by heard screams coming from the mill-yard, where Mrs. Palmer used to flog her slaves unmercifully and submit them to brutal forms of torture for the most trivial offences; how she would beat the females on their naked backs with a perforated patter which drew blood, and how she would compel them to wear shoes the soles of which were studded on the inside with sharp wooden pegs. To strangers her demeanour would be affable and kind, and it was only when they heard the shrieks of her victims and saw the objects of torture that they could believe the extent of the enormities which she committed.

Then the time came when the slaves could stand it no longer and entered into a conspiracy to rid themselves of their mistress. The opportunity was soon at hand. One day in the Great House at Palmyra, when, in a paroxysm of rage, she was attacking a young negro with a whip, the boy turned on her and seized her by the throat. Other slaves rushed up and forcing her to the ground smothered her with a mattress, on which they trampled till the last breath left her body.

An inquiry was held by a neighbouring magistrate, but no act of violence was proved, and it was not until some years afterwards that the truth was known by the confession of a dying slave, who also alleged that Mr. Palmer was a consenting party to the murder.

Mrs. Palmer was buried in the pasture of the Great

House in which she died. It was with difficulty that any one could be found to dig her grave. Indeed, it is said that it was only by the offer of a bribe of a calf that a negro was persuaded to perform this office.

According to a pamphlet issued by Mr. Castello, a monument was erected to Mrs. Palmer in Montego Bay Church, "of the purest white, without a speck or blemish," ornamented with " a broken pillar, an over-turned lamp, a dead tree, a declining headstone, a setting sun and a skull, artistically grouped together." Of this no trace whatever remains, and it seems incredible that any one could have wished to perpetuate the memory of such a woman by the erection of a monument, or that the Rector could have permitted a memorial to her to be raised in his church.

Apart from its romantic history Rose Hall has, by reason of its glorious position and by reason, too, of the fact that it is so typical of the " Great Houses " in which the planters lived in the days of King Sugar, a remarkable fascination and charm, and one cannot visit it without feeling that it deserves a less cruel fate than that which has now befallen it. It would be better if some enterprising individual were to acquire it and turn it into an hotel than that it should be allowed to fall into decay and ruin.

APPENDIX

I

THE WILL OF GOVERNOR DANIEL PARKE

THE last will and testament of the unhappy Governor Daniel Parke is perhaps of sufficient interest to merit reproduction. It is given in "Antigua and the Antiguans" as follows :

" In the name of God, Amen. I, Daniel Parke, Capt.-Gen. and Chief Governor, &c., of all the Leeward Islands, make this, my last Will and Testament, in manner following : (Imprimis, I bequeath my soul to Almighty God.) I give all my estate in these islands, both land and houses, negroes, debts, and so forth, to Thos. Long, Esq. and Mister Ceasar Rodney, for the use of Mistress Lucy Chester, being the daughter of Mistress Katharine Chester,* though she is not yet christened, and if her mother thinks fit to call her after any other name, I still doe bequeath all my estate in the four islands of my government to her ; but in case she dies before she attains the age of twenty-one years, then I bequeath the same to her mother, Mistress

---

* Wife of Edward Chester, Esq.

Katharine Chester, that it shall be and remain in the
hands of my loving friends, Collonel Thos. Long and
Mister Ceaser Rodney, the produce of the same to be
paid into her own hands, but to no other person whatsoever, and after the decease of the said Mistress
Katharine Chester, then I bequeath the same to my godson, Julius Ceasar Parke, and his heirs for ever, but in
case the said youngest daughter of the said Mistress
Katharine Chester lives to marry and have children, I
give the whole to her eldest son, and the heirs male of
his body, and for the want of such heirs, to her second
son's son, and the heirs of his body, and for want of such,
to her next, and so on to her heir, provided still, he that
heirs itt, calls himself by the name of Parke ; and my
will is, that the said youngest daughter of Mistress
Katharine Chester alter her name, and that she calls her-
self by the name of Parke, and that whosoever shall
marry her, calls himself by the name of Parke, and that
she and the heirs of her body, themselves by the name
of Parke, and use my coat of arms which is yet of my
family of the county of Essex, but in case she refuses, or
her heirs, to call themselves by the name of Parke, then
my will is, that all my estate, both real and personal, go
to my godson, Julius Ceaser Parke, to him and the heirs
of his body for ever, and for want of such heirs, to the
heirs of my daughter Francis Curtis, and for want of
such heirs, to the heirs of the body of my daughter Lucy
Bird, always provided whoever shall enjoy this my estate,
shall call themselves by the names of Parke.

"Item, I give to my daughter Francis Curtis, all my
estate, both real and personal, either in Virginia or
248

England, and the heirs of her body, provided they shall
call themselves by the name of Parke, and for want of
such heirs, to the heirs of the body of my daughter Lucy
Bird, and for want of such heirs, to the heirs of the body
of the youngest daughter, now living, of Mistress Katharine Chester, and for want of such heirs, to the heirs of
the body of Julius Ceasar Parke, provided still, that whoever has this my estate shall call themselves by the name
of Parke, and that in case of failure of heirs, or that they
refuse to call themselves by the name of Parke, then my
Will is, that my estate go to the poor of the parish of
White Church, in Hampshire, but my Will is, that my
daughter Francis Curtis pay out of my estate in Hampshire and Virginia, the following legacies and all my
debts, that is, to my daughter Lucy Bird, one thousand
pounds sterling; to my godson Julius Ceasar Parke,
fifty pounds sterling each year during his life; to my
three sisters and their children, fifty pounds to buy them
rings; and to my Executors, hereafter named in England, each twenty pounds, and my Will is, that Thos.
Long, Esq. of this island, and Mister Ceasar Rodney,
and Major Saml. Byam, be my Executors in trust for
the performance of what is to be done with my estate in
the Leeward Islands; and that Micajah Perry, Esq.,
Mister Thomas Laws, and Mr. Richard Perry, of
London, merchant, to be Executors in trust for the performance of what is to be done in England and Virginia,
and I doe hereby Revoke all former Wills, Declaring
this to be my last Will and Testamen., being writ with
all my owne hand, signed and sealed in St. John's, in
Antigua, the Twenty-ninth day of January, in the year

of our Lord, One thousand seven hundred nine and ten.

" Sealed, published, and Declared to be his Will and Testament, } DANIEL PARKE.

" In the presence of us,

" HERBERT PEMBER,
" JOHN BIRMINGHAM,
" WILLIAM MARTIN."

" December the seventh, One thousand seven hundred and ten, I doe appoint in the room of Collonel Thos. Long, deceased, Mister Abraham Redwood to be one of my Executors in trust, to see this my will performed.

" DANIEL PARKE."

II

ARTICLES OF CAPITULATION OF THE ISLAND OF ST. CHRISTOPHER'S, between his Excellency the Count de Grasse, the Marquis de Bouillé, Major-General Shirley, Governor, and Brigadier-General Fraser.

" ARTICLE 1. The governor, the commander of the troops, the regular officers and soldiers, the officers and privates of militia, shall march through the breach on the fort of Brimstone Hill with all the honours of war, with drums beating, colours flying, one mortar, two

250

field-pieces, ten rounds each, arms and baggage, and then lay down their arms at a place appointed, the officers excepted.

" 2. The regular troops shall be prisoners of war, and sent to England in safe and good vessels, which shall be furnished with provisions for the voyage; but they shall not serve against the King of France until they shall be exchanged. The officers are permitted to reside in any of the islands upon their parole. The militia and armed negroes shall return to their respective homes.

" 3. The inhabitants, or their attornies, shall be obliged to take the oaths of fidelity to the King of France, within the space of one month, before the governor of the said islands; and those that are prevented from it by sickness shall obtain a delay.

" 4. They shall observe an exact neutrality, and shall not be compelled to take up arms against His Britannic Majesty, or any other power. They are at liberty to retain their arms, for the internal police and better subjection of their negroes; but they are to make a return of them to the justices of the peace, who shall be responsible for any bad use that may be made of them contrary to the tenor of the present capitulation.

" 5. They shall enjoy, until a peace, their laws, customs, and ordinances. Justice shall be administered by the same persons who are actually in office. All expences attending the administration of justice shall be defrayed by the colony.

" 6. The court of chancery shall be held by the council of the island, and in the same form as hereto-

251

fore; and all appeals from the said court shall be made to His most Christian Majesty in council.

" 7. The inhabitants and clergy shall be supported in the possession of their estates and properties of whatsoever nature or denomination, and in their privileges, rights, titles, honours, and exemptions, and in the possession of their religion and their ministers in the enjoyment of their livings. The absentees, and those who are in the service of His Britannic Majesty, shall be maintained in the possession and enjoyment of their estates and properties, which shall be managed by their attornies. The inhabitants may sell their estates and possessions to whom they shall think proper, and they are at liberty to send their children to England to be educated, and from whence they may return when they judge proper.

" 8. The inhabitants shall pay monthly, into the hands of the treasurer of the troops, in lieu of all taxes, the value of two-thirds of the articles that the island of St. Christopher's and Nevis paid to the King of Great Britain, which he shall estimate according to the valuation of the revenues made in the year 1781, and which shall serve as a basis.

" 9. The stores which may have been taken during the siege shall be religiously restored, and they may also be reclaimed in one of the French Windward and Leeward Islands.

" 10. The inhabitants shall not be obliged to furnish the troops with quarters, except in extraordinary cases; but they are to be lodged at the expence of the King, or in houses belonging to the Crown.

" 11. In cases where the King's business may require negroes to work, they shall be furnished by the inhabitants of the said islands in the number of 500, but they shall be paid at the rate of two 'bills' (bitts) per day each, and victualled at the expence of the King.

" 12. The vessels and droghers belonging to the inhabitants at the capitulation shall be restored to their owners.

The vessels which the said inhabitants expected from the ports of England, or from any of His Britannic Majesty's possessions, shall be received in the said colonies during the space of six months; and they may load them to return under neutral colours, even for the ports of Great Britain, with the particular permission of the governor; and if any of the vessels expected shall stop at any of the English islands, the governor shall be authorised to grant permission for them to come to either of the aforesaid islands.

" 13. The inhabitants and merchants shall enjoy all the privileges of commerce granted to the subjects of His most Christian Majesty throughout all the extent of his dominions.

" 14. Whatever may have been furnished for the French army during the siege and to this day by the said islands, and the losses that the inhabitants have sustained by the burning of plantations, and by every other means, shall be estimated by a meeting of the inhabitants, and the amount equally borne by the two islands, under the head of contribution or indemnity for the expences of the war; but in such a manner, that this article shall not diminish the taxes above mentioned, which are to take place from the date of the capitulation ; but the assembly of the inhabitants may apply to it the arrears of the general taxes which remain in their hands at the date of capitulation.

"15. The sailors of merchant ships, those of privateers, and other individuals who have no property in the said islands, shall depart from the same in the space of six weeks, if they are not employed in droghers, or avowed by two proprietors, who will answer for them, and means shall be furnished for them to depart for the neutral islands.

"16. The general of the French troops shall be put in possession of all the artillery, all the effects depending on the colonies belonging to His Britannic Majesty, all powder, arms, ammunition, and King's vessels, shall be given to the commander of the French troops, and an inventory of them presented to the governor.

"17. Out of respect to the courage and determined conduct of Generals Shirley and Fraser, we consent that they shall not be considered as prisoners of war, but the former may return to his government of Antigua, and the latter may continue in the service of his country, being happy to testify this mark of particular esteem for those brave officers.

It is moreover covenanted, that the inhabitants of these islands, with the permission of the governor, may export their merchandise in neutral vessels for all the ports of France and America.

LE MARQUIS DE BOUILLÉ,
THOMAS SHIRLEY,
THOMAS FRASER, Brig.-Gen.

APPENDIX III

III

THE LOSS OF THE DIAMOND ROCK

THE following is the full text of Captain J. W. Maurice's letter to Rear-Admiral Cochrane giving an account of the loss of the Diamond Rock, which was read at the court-martial on board H.M.S. *Circe*, in Carlisle Bay, Barbados, on June 24th, 1805 :

SIR,   BARBADOES, *June* 19, 1805.

In my letter of the 14th May, to Sir Francis Lafforey, I informed him of the arrival of the enemy's combined squadron off the Rock, and of our having had one hour's partial action with them as they passed it : their force consisting of sixteen sail of the line, eight frigates, three brigs, one armed en flute, and His Majesty's late sloop Cyanne.

On the 16th of May, at half-past seven in the morning, saw a large ship rounding Point Saline, and from her appearance I plainly saw she was a ship of the line, and from the cut of her sails an enemy. At eight she hoisted a Spanish ensign and pendant ; I immediately directed French colours to be hoisted as a decoy, which fully answered my wishes, for at twenty minutes before nine she had got under the lee of the Rock, at the distance of three quarters of a mile, when I shifted the colours, and opened a well directed fire of round and grape from Fort Diamond ; the first shot striking her under the fore channels, she directly put her helm up, and in the act of wearing returned one feeble shot. From the little winds she did not get out of the range of shot until nine, but continued running before the wind until twelve. At two an enemy's brig stood out of Port Royal, and beat to windward of the Rock, where she continued to cruise. I was now fully satisfied in my own mind of the intention of the enemy to attack the Rock. From the 16th to the 29th the Rock was completely blockaded by frigates, brigs, schooners, and small boats, sloop-rigged, which prevented any supplies being thrown in to me; for on the 25th a sloop from St. Lucia, with my second Lieutenant, who had carried dispatches to Barbadoes, and the Purser, who had gone over to complete the provisions to four months, were taken under my guns, endeavouring to throw in some barrels of powder, although we covered her with a spirited fire from Fort Diamond, Centaur's Battery, and Maurice's Battery. On the 29th, at half past five in the evening, two ships of the line, one frigate, and a schooner, with 11 gun-boats in tow, stood out from Fort Royal, under all sail. I now had not the smallest doubt that the squadron was intended for the attack of the Diamond. The Rock was put into the best state of defence it could, as far as little ammunition and water would allow; but I was determined to defend it while I had any remaining. On the 30th, at sunrise, the enemy's squadron had fallen far to leeward; but the wind unfortunately veering very much to the southward, (indeed farther than I had known it for some months,) enabled them to fetch as high as St. Ann's Bay, where they continued under easy sail for the night. On the morning of the 31st, at sunrise, they were still under easy sail, far to windward; but from the number of their signals, and having cast off their boats, I was convinced the attack would be made soon. At seven the enemy bore up in a line for the Rock, the gun-boats, &c. keeping within them, crowded with troops. Seeing the impossibility of defending the lower works against such a force, and the certainty of our being prevented from gaining the heights without considerable loss, and which could not be defended for any time without us, with the greatest reluctance I ordered the whole above the first lodgement, having a man at each gun to give the enemy their discharge, which they did, and joined me over the North Garden Pass, excepting the cook, who was made a prisoner. What powder was left below we drowned, and cut away the launch, that she might not be serviceable to the enemy. At ten minutes before eight we had every person up, and the ladders secured, when the Berwick opened her fire within pistol shot, and at eight the whole of the enemy's squadron of ships and gun-boats were in action, which was returned by Hood's Battery and Fort Diamond; the whole of the troops in the boats keeping up a heavy fire of musketry. It was a fortunate circumstance we quitted the lower works when we did, as our own stones hove down by the enemy's shot would have killed and wounded the whole of us. I was now busily employed in placing the people on the different lodgements, with small arms, to harrass the enemy as they landed, and cover themselves. I am happy to say that the execution done was considerable; for the fire of our men was so galling, that the seamen left their boats, excepting three men in each, who were shot dead, and three of the gun-boats went adrift ; two of them went on shore at Martinique, and were beat to pieces, and the other went to sea. The whole of the enemy's squadron were constantly employed during this day in bombarding the Rock, as they could fetch in to windward of it. At night the whole of the men were posted on different lodgements, to harrass the enemy as they threw in supplies and reinforcements : on the 1st the enemy's squadron employed constantly bombarding the Rock, the fire from the troops much more spirited : on the 2nd the enemy's squadron bombarding as before, who had been reinforced with another brig, but the fire from the troops this day very severe, as they had during the night got under the rocks in the surf, and were covered by the overhanging rocks, and as our men appeared they fired up. At four in the afternoon, on examining into our ammunition, I found we had but little powder left, and not a sufficient quantity of ball cartridges to last until dark, and being firmly of opinion the enemy meant to endeavour to carry the heights by assault that night, I thought it a duty I owed to those brave fellows who had so gallantly supported me during three days and two nights constant battle, to offer terms of capitulation ; and having consulted my first Lieutenant, who was of the same opinion, at half-past four, the unhappiest moment of my life, I threw out a flag of truce, which returned at five, with honourable terms for the garrison, and the next morning we embarked on board the Pluton and Berwick, and on the fourth we were sent to Barbadoes in a cartel, agreeable

258

to the articles, except fourteen men, which they forcibly detained unknown to me, getting men to swear they were French. I have written to Captain Kempt, Agent for prisoners of war, stating the business, as well as their endeavouring to entice the whole of my crew to enter into their service, but, thank God! I trust no Englishman, let him be ever so bad, is base enough to do it. I beg leave to recommend in the strongest terms, the able and gallant support I received from my first Lieutenant, Mr. Robert Adams Wadham, and whose services at different times in carrying dispatches to Barbadoes, relating to the enemy, merits my warmest acknowledgments. I am also much indebted to Lieutenant Watson, of the marines, for his active and able support. Those, Sir, were the only officers I had, but I needed not more, for the conduct of the whole of my people was so active, orderly, and gallant, that I shall always reflect on it with pleasure to the latest day of my life. Indeed, when you observe that we had only two killed and one wounded, you will perceive, that had not my orders been put in execution with the greatest promptness and attention, we must have met with great loss ; and had I let loose their valour, I should have lost half my men. Their fatigue and hardships are beyond description, having only a pint of water during 24 hours, under a vertical sun, and not a moment's rest day or night ; and several of them fainted for want of water, and obliged to drink their own. A schooner had brought out sixty scaling ladders, to attempt us that night under cover of the ships, and four more ships of the line were to have come against us the next day.

APPENDIX III

Indeed the whole of the combined squadron's launches were employed on the service, and not less than three thousand men. The Captain of the Sireine frigate was wounded through the knee. My only consolation is, that although I unfortunately lost the Rock, I trust its defence was honourable, and hope it will merit your approbation.

I have the honour to remain

Your most humble and obedient Servant,

J. W. MAURICE.